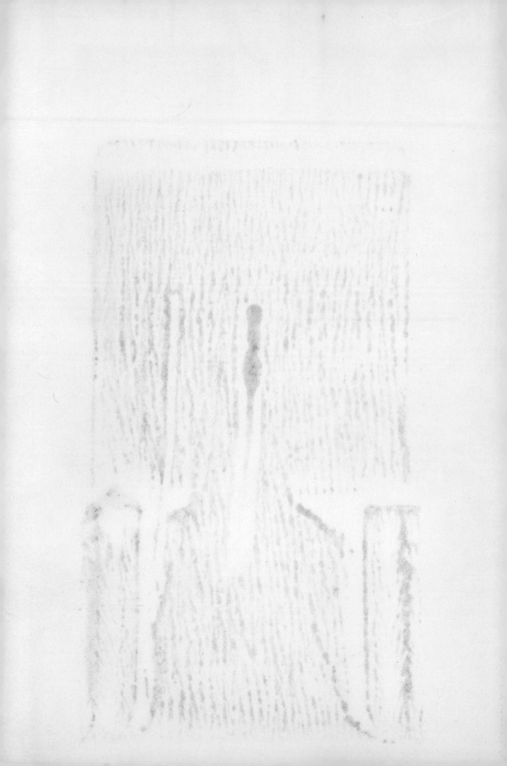

TEST BAN AND DISARMAMENT:
The Path of Negotiation

TEST BAN AND DISARMAMENT:
The Path of Negotiation

by ARTHUR H. DEAN

Published *for the*
Council on Foreign Relations
by
Harper & Row, Publishers
New York and London

The Council on Foreign Relations is a non-profit institution devoted to the study of political, economic, and strategic problems as related to American foreign policy. It takes no stand, expressed or implied, on American policy.

The authors of books published under the auspices of the Council are responsible for their statements of fact and expressions of opinion. The Council is responsible only for determining that they should be presented to the public.

For a list of Council publications see pages 151-153

TEST BAN AND DISARMAMENT:
THE PATH OF NEGOTIATION

FIRST EDITION

Library of Congress catalog card number: 66-15737
Printed in the United States of America
Published by Harper & Row, Publishers, Incorporated
B-Q

To M.M.D.
with many thanks
for her warm interest
and understanding

IN MEMORY OF EDWARD JOHN NOBLE

The Policy Book series of the Council on Foreign Relations is published under a grant from the Edward John Noble Foundation in memory of Mr. Noble and his interest in encouraging American leadership.

Policy Books of the Council on Foreign Relations

Disarmament, all governments publicly agree, is a necessary and desirable goal if the world is to have any assurance of peace and security. How to get there, how even to make a modest start, is anything but agreed. Years of negotiation have achieved very little in the way of international accord in this field. Yet those negotiations cannot be dismissed as useless. They have brought a greater understanding of how the questions of nuclear testing and disarmament are woven into the total fabric of international politics. They have clarified the problems which confront the United States, above all in the relations between the Western nations and the Soviet Union. The paucity of concrete results only points up the continued urgency of controlling nuclear weapons and preventing their spread to other nations beyond the few which now possess them.

The subject is as complex as it is important. Volumes have been written on it. The main elements, however, and the policy considerations which flow from them seem peculiarly suited to the format of the series of short Policy Books of the Council on Foreign Relations. These books have a twofold purpose: first, to provide readers in this country and elsewhere with essays and analytical studies of the highest quality on problems of world significance; and second, to contribute to constructive thinking on American policies of the future. They are deliberately kept brief, not with the aim of simplification but to present with a minimum of factual background and detail the reasoned conclusions of individual authors with special experience and qualifications.

Arthur H. Dean, the author of this volume, has had incomparable experience both in negotiation and in the general field of American foreign relations. In recent years he has rendered distinguished service to the administrations of Presidents Eisenhower, Kennedy, and Johnson in a number of capacities. His experience as ambassador charged with negotiating on disarmament and the nuclear test ban at Geneva and elsewhere uniquely qualifies him to interpret the meaning of those negotiations and to express views on what is at stake in the future. The Council was indeed fortunate in persuading him to undertake this book.

In the course of preparing his manuscript Mr. Dean had the valuable assistance of Mrs. Marina S. Finkelstein, for whose expert research and drafting both he and the Council owe a large debt of gratitude. In the later stages, an expert group met at the Council to discuss the manuscript with the author. The Council wishes to thank the following, who were present at that meeting: Bernhard G. Bechhoefer, Franklin Long, Philip E. Mosely, Nedville Nordness, Charles P. Noyes, David H. Popper, and George Rathjens.

This is Mr. Dean's book. The views and conclusions are his own, not those of the Council on Foreign Relations or of any group. The Council takes responsibility for the decision to publish it as a significant contribution to thought on questions vital to the survival of the world as we know it.

JOHN C. CAMPBELL
Editor

Preface

Two basic reasons underlie the writing of this book. The first is the urgency and importance of curbing the arms race, preventing the spread of nuclear weapons, and reaching a comprehensive nuclear test-ban treaty with an effective verification and identification system. The danger of uncontrolled competition in modern weapons of terrific destructive power is all too apparent. Moreover, the exploding world population, the impending food crisis, the terrific destructiveness of modern warfare, and the acute problems facing the developing countries point to the absurdity of spending more than $200 billion per annum on arms, a sum larger than the combined national income of all the underdeveloped countries in the free world.

The second reason is the need to put this subject in a realistic light. These are not problems that well-intentioned people will solve by enthusiastic advocacy of general and complete disarmament, without thinking through the practical process of balanced and phased arms control and reduction, including essential inspection and verification measures, and without taking full account of the practical problems that would still remain in a disarming or disarmed world in which there is really no true communication, as we understand it, with the Soviet mind, let alone the thinking of the Chinese Communists. Nor will these problems be solved by unilateral gestures and declarations on the part of the United States government, for we have seen that words, gestures, and unilateral concessions do not influence the basic policies of Moscow or of Peking.

There is a need in this country for greater understanding of what the real questions are and how they can be solved. The experience of international negotiation on the nuclear test ban and on disarmament over the past few years, in which I have had the honor to take part and which provides most of the raw material for this book, should contribute to that greater understanding. It gives an idea of the technical complexities of the problem itself, and of what is actually involved in the process of seeking agreement and then making the agreement work.

Imaginative and bold thinking is essential to progress toward arms control and disarmament. But concrete achievement will require long, hard, and patient work and objective recognition of the scientific and the political obstacles and of the relationship between them. To ignore these realities is to deceive ourselves and to do a disservice to all free nations.

In the course of public service and in the development of my own thinking on these matters I have had the benefit of advice and assistance from many sources. I wish, first of all, to express my deep appreciation of the confidence, encouragement, and unfailing support of the late President Kennedy. My thanks go also to Secretary of State Dean Rusk; Under Secretary George Ball; Secretary of Defense Robert McNamara and former Deputy Secretary of Defense Roswell L. Gilpatric; McGeorge Bundy, Special Assistant to Presidents Kennedy and Johnson for National Security Affairs; the late Adlai E. Stevenson, former U. S. Representative to the United Nations; Francis T. P. Plimpton and Charles Yost, U.S. Deputy Representatives to the United Nations; Jerome B. Wiesner, Special Science Adviser to President Kennedy; Herbert F. York, Science Adviser to the Department of Defense under President Eisenhower; Glenn Seaborg, Chairman of the Atomic Energy Commission; Allen W. Dulles and John A. McCone, former Directors of the Central Intelligence Agency; the National Science Foundation and its Director, Leland J. Haworth; the Joint Chiefs of Staff; John J. McCloy, Disarmament Adviser to President Kennedy; William C. Foster, Director of the Arms Control and Disarmament Agency; the author's former deputy Adrian S. Fisher, now Deputy Director of ACDA; his former Special Assistant George W. Rathjens; Jacob Beam, Herbert Scoville, Jr., and Archibald S. Alexander, Assistant Directors of ACDA; and its general counsel George Bunn; Franklin A. Long, former Assistant Director of ACDA for Science and Technology; Congressman Chet Holifield and Senator John O. Pastore, Chairmen of the Joint Committee on Atomic Energy; Vice President Hubert Humphrey in his former capacity as Chairman of the Senate Foreign Relations Committee's Subcommittee on Disarmament; the late Charles C. Stelle, the author's very able deputy; John McNaughton, Assistant Secretary of Defense for International Affairs; Senators Clark, Fulbright, and Sparkman; Lord Harlech (formerly Sir David Ormsby-Gore), Joseph Godber and Sir Michael Wright of the British Delegation at Geneva; General E. L. M. Burns of the Canadian Delegation; and Francesco Cavelletti of the Italian Delegation; Alex Akalovsky; Vincent Baker; Charles J. Davis; Frederic A. Fisher; Raymond Garthoff; William Gehron; Betty Goetz (now Mrs. Arthur Lall); James Goodby; Dr. Warren Heckrotte of the Lawrence Radiation Laboratory; Colonel Carl Johnson; Spurgeon M. Keeny, Jr.; Anne W. Marks; the late Edward R. Murrow, head of the United States Information Agency; Nedville Nordness; Doyle L. Northrup, Director of the AFTAC; Thomas Pickering; Arthur Barber; David H. Popper; David E. Mark; Ronald Spiers; Robert G. Sturgill; Lawrence Weiler; Ernest G. Wiener; and Ernest H. Wiener, Jr. I am especially indebted to those who reviewed the manuscript with me at an all-day meeting at the Council on Foreign Relations.

I am grateful also to my secretaries, Gertrude Horner and Carole Manzo, and to my wife for her patient understanding of the task involved.

Mrs. Marina S. Finkelstein gave me invaluable assistance in work on the manuscript, and John C. Campbell and Robert Valkenier of the staff of the Council on Foreign Relations were helpful in editing and preparing it for publication. The basic responsibility for the ideas expressed remains with the author.

A. H. D.

New York
December, 1965

Contents

PREFACE ix

I INTRODUCTION 1

II DISARMAMENT DIPLOMACY 18

III VERIFICATION AND INSPECTION 49

IV DISARMAMENT AND ARMS CONTROL 63

V NUCLEAR TEST-BAN TREATY 81

VI POINTS OF EMPHASIS 107

VII THE URGENT FUTURE 120

NOTE ON EARTHQUAKES AND UNDERGROUND
EXPLOSIONS 139

INDEX 145

TEST BAN AND DISARMAMENT:
The Path of Negotiation

Chapter I

Introduction

In the late afternoon of a lovely summer day in June 1928, the author was having tea in a beautiful Japanese garden facing west with Sir Kengo Mori, financial advisor to the Japanese government, Baron Shidehara, former Japanese Ambassador to the United States and later the Foreign Minister, the Swedish Minister to Japan, and Boris A. Bakhmetieff, the last ambassador from pre-Soviet Russia to the United States. Sir Kengo Mori had raised the question whether Japan should adhere to the pact just proposed by the American Secretary of State, Frank Kellogg, and the Foreign Minister of France, Aristide Briand, which provided for the "renunciation of war as an instrument of national policy," the so-called Pact of Paris.

In the contemporary Far Eastern setting, Chang Tso-lin, the famous war lord of Manchuria, had been assassinated only a few weeks before outside Mukden, under suspicious circumstances to say the least. In China proper, the forces of Chiang Kai-shek, leader of the Kuomintang and successor of Sun Yat-sen, were engaged in civil war with other nationalist and war-lord armies, as they moved slowly north from Nanking toward Peking. Chiang had broken with Borodin, Stalin's emissary, and the Comintern in the previous year, and Mao Tse-tung was attempting to reorganize the Chinese Communist forces in Kwangtung and Hunan provinces. Meanwhile, the relations of the Chinese with the Western powers were in a state of recurring crisis marked by frequent incidents of Chinese firing on British and American gunboats on the Yangtze.

The question raised by Sir Kengo Mori was whether, in view of the troubled and uncertain situation in China and Manchuria, where Japan had more than a quarter-million nationals and vast investments, and in view of the Communist control of Russia and Siberia down to the Manchurian border, Japan could in all good conscience, without being accused of hypocrisy, sign the proposed Kellogg-Briand Pact to outlaw war.

Ambassador Bakhmetieff fetched a large silk handkerchief from his breast pocket, took off his old-fashioned pince-nez glasses, and while polishing them and squinting into the western sun, began to speak in the following vein.

"Of course you must sign," he said. "No one will understand it if you do not. Everyone will accuse you of being a warmonger. Your country faces a terrible dilemma. In Russia, the Bolshevists are building a new society of which I fundamentally disapprove. But as a member of the *ancien régime* I know it is gone forever. And make no mistake, the Bolshevists have a powerful army and will follow Russian national policy in Siberia, Manchuria, and the control of its railway to the warm-weather ports at Dairen and Port Arthur.

"The old traditional society in China is rapidly disintegrating. There are generations of trouble ahead for you in China and Manchuria. India and Indo-China are in a state of ferment. The English, French, and Dutch will lose their colonial empires. Change is in the air.

"You should, of course, do everything you can to avoid war. War solves nothing and is the bankruptcy of diplomacy. Great Britain and France are supposed to have defeated Germany in the recent war. But they were both bled white in manpower and resources. Germany was defeated. She has lost her colonies. But her industrial power has been completely modernized with the aid of American loans and she is looking forward, not backward. Stresemann and the German Weimar Republic cannot stand up against the Junkers and industrialists. Briand, though he wants peace, distrusts Germany too much to cooperate effectively. On the whole he is negative, which never pays off.

"The Kellogg-Briand Pact itself is meaningless. It cannot work. It is merely an unenforceable declaration of intent. It has no organization or machinery to police or to enforce it. The League of Nations is an empty debating society.

"Rulers of nations have grave responsibilities to their people. They cannot rely merely on good intentions. They must have the ability and the intention to act. In diplomacy he who relies on good intentions alone will ride a bony nag and will be doomed to disappointment. Diplomacy requires careful planning and readily recognizable power to back it up."

Turning to me, he said, "Young man, your country is a rising power. Your people are very generous of their great resources. But you will be drawn inevitably, whether you like it or not, into the power vortex, as the French, British, and Dutch power goes down. And you will find that moralistic pacts made with fervor but without reality will only deceive and mislead people. They do great harm.

"Your country cannot continue to set moral standards for international conduct and at the same time disclaim all responsibility for the enforcement of your moral intentions. You make a great mistake in making grandiose statements such as your "Open Door Policy" on China of Secretary Hay in 1900 and your recent Nine-Power Treaty of 1922. You insisted on the principle of the territorial integrity of China in each statement. Then you signed disarmament agreements along with the Nine-Power Treaty which rendered you militarily impotent to enforce your principles.

"You must realize that with their very difficult problems elsewhere the British and the French cannot and will not help you enforce your moralistic statements on China. They have other axes to grind. If your so-called Kellogg-Briand Peace Pact is violated, as it will be, you can do nothing but wring your hands and moan at the wickedness of the world. When you are responsible for the peace, you will be the wicked one.

"If you cannot enforce moralistic agreements, then do not make them. Metternich may have been a Machiavelli but he kept the peace of Europe."

Norman Armour and Eugene Dooman, Counselor and First Secretary, respectively, of the American Embassy in Tokyo, had asked me to say a good word for the Kellogg-Briand Pact to my

Japanese friends, if I had the opportunity. But after this penetrating statement I decided to wait for a more propitious occasion. Bakhmetieff's words made a profound impression upon me. I often pondered and reflected on them.

As a young lawyer I had worked briefly with Frank Kellogg, our Secretary of State under President Coolidge. He was a distinguished and able lawyer from St. Paul, Minnesota, a fine Christian gentleman of great moral integrity. But he had had no previous foreign or diplomatic experience and as a middle westerner distrusted international organizations such as the League of Nations or its adjunct the World Court.

In the course of my career I have often acted as a lawyer or negotiator for corporations or banking interests abroad and have constantly been impressed with the need for clear and objective analysis, patient and unemotional examination of pertinent economic and political facts, and the absolute necessity of working out ahead of time how organizations are to be set up and controlled, and how they will work and function, particularly in time of stress. When this is not done carefully in advance, there is sure to be trouble. One can depend on it.

The terrible destruction of World War II culminating in the dropping of the two atomic bombs in August 1945 on Japan, a country in which I had many friends because of my work there in 1927-28, made a deep imprint on my mind. The enormous damage, the maiming and the loss of lives, convinced me that it was imperative to set up new, workable, and effective machinery for peace, in our own interests if for no other reason.

Our government had taken a leading role in the establishment of the United Nations. But when the new organization was set up in San Francisco in the spring of 1945, with power divided between the Security Council and the General Assembly, and with the United States, the U.S.S.R., Great Britain, France, and China as permanent members of the Security Council with the right of veto, the delegates were not aware of the awesome atomic weapon and its capability of vast destruction; they could not know that Soviet power would entrench itself in Central Europe and reach out for further conquests, that the Communists would overrun the mainland of China in 1949, that the British, French,

Belgian, and Dutch empires would be stripped of their colonial possessions, that the original fifty-two members of the United Nations would grow to well over one hundred, that the U.S.S.R. would use its veto power in the Security Council so often, or that the United States, Great Britain, the U.S.S.R., France, and Communist China would become nuclear powers.

During the years that followed, the proliferation of nuclear weapons and the world's inability to agree on their control preyed on my mind. From 1958 to 1960 my good friend Ambassador James J. Wadsworth was heading our delegation at the Conference on the Discontinuance of Nuclear Weapons Tests in Geneva. Twice in that period I represented the United States at the Conferences on the Law of the Sea in that same city. He and I had often talked of this problem of nuclear weapons and of its possible solution.

One afternoon in late 1958 at a reception a young mother said to me that she was afraid to bear any more children because of the contamination of the air by nuclear testing and because of the possible destruction of the world by nuclear weapons. I tried to assure her that nuclear testing would be stopped and nuclear weapons brought under control. She turned and said, "Well, what are you doing about it? Why are you so sure this problem will be solved? What assurance do you really have to offer?"

I thought often about her words and continued to study the problem. But what was I really doing to help?

So, when President Kennedy in January 1961, through his Special Adviser on Disarmament, John J. McCloy, asked me to work with him on the proposed nuclear test-ban treaty and on disarmament, I responded gladly and hoped I could be of some service both to my country and to mankind.

For some two years during the administration of President Kennedy, I served as chairman of the U.S. delegation at the disarmament and nuclear test-ban negotiations in Geneva, as a member of our delegation to the General Assembly of the United Nations, and in Washington. During this time, I was especially concerned with three matters: first, aiding Mr. McCloy in the drafting of the statute for the Arms Control and Disarmament Agency as an essential domestic instrument for the formulation of policy in this field; second, the development and presentation of our proposals on general and complete disarmament at the United Nations in September 1961 and at Geneva in April 1962; and third, the drafting and negotiation of the nuclear test-ban treaty at Geneva in 1961 and 1962 and its separation in August 1962 into two versions, comprehensive and partial, the latter forming the basis for the treaty signed in Moscow on August 5, 1963. Later, in 1964, I was called to serve as an adviser to President Johnson on foreign affairs and on his Special Committee on the Proliferation of Nuclear Weapons. The experiences of these years are the seedbed for the pages which follow.

Working on disarmament, necessary as it is, can seem at times as fruitless as trying to punch holes in water. Weeks and months may go by with all proposals meeting not the slightest positive response from the Soviet side. But, given the modern condition in which major war would mean a world-wide disaster, it is vitally important to make the continuing effort to reach acceptable agreements even when the political obstacles make continued negotiation discouraging. The mere process of talking, exploring, and questioning may in itself have certain positive results.

The year 1961, it may be recalled, did not open with any high prospects for achieving progress toward disarmament. Our immediate task was to see whether the talks on general disarmament at Geneva, which had been disrupted by the Soviet walkout from the Ten-Nation Conference in June 1960, could be resumed. By March 1961 it was possible to announce the encouraging development that private bilateral talks with Soviet representatives would begin, in the hope of clearing away the roadblocks to a new series of negotiations. During the same month, however, the Soviet Union set back our hopes by introducing in the nuclear test-ban talks a "troika" proposal that would have stultified the operation of the proposed international control organ. Since a similar arrangement had already been discussed by the United States and the United Kingdom in 1958 and rejected, and since even the Soviet Union had assented to an alternative approach, the Soviet reversion to an abandoned position did not make for immediate optimism.

In spite of these setbacks, and in spite also of the rebuffs which

were to follow when—in the atmosphere of crisis over Berlin—
the Soviet Union broke off the promising test-ban talks at the
end of August 1961 and began its long and secretly planned
series of nuclear tests in the atmosphere, it was a truly stimulating time to be working on disarmament questions as a representative of our government. The effort to reach agreements by
negotiation had been steadily pursued during the administration
of President Eisenhower, for whom I had great admiration and
under whom I served three times as an ambassador—in the postarmistice negotiations in Korea and twice at the Conference on
the Law of the Sea in 1958 and 1960. But one sensed in early
1961 a new drive and sense of determination, sparked by the
enthusiasm of President Kennedy himself. He wanted, as he
phrased it in his inaugural address, to begin anew the quest for
peace and to do this together with those nations which "would
make themselves our adversary," especially, of course, with the
Soviet Union.

In this quest for honorable agreements that would not sacrifice
national interests, but rather would serve them, the President
believed that the field of disarmament and arms control would
be a good place to start even though the record was not encouraging. His first goal was to try to break the log jam by reaching
some limited agreement in that field. Even a minor success there
might lead to broader agreements on disarmament or on political
questions.

At the same time, President Kennedy wanted a broad survey, a
reassessment of our entire policy on disarmament and arms control. With that belief in the overriding power of human intelligence and will which was so characteristic of the man, he wanted
it conducted with sober attention to facts but also with verve,
imagination, flexibility, and a positive and forward intent. For
he disliked negativism. He wanted us to pull the various parts of
policy together into a coherent whole, identify its lacks and gaps,
and remedy them. He wanted his representatives to seize opportunities and not to be afraid of modifying proposals in the light
of scientific advances and of changing political circumstances. He
communicated a lively personal interest; remained easily and
readily available for consultation when needed; read the dis-

patches from Geneva, the scientific reports, and the draft proposals himself; and wanted results.

We who undertook this assignment felt that disarmament and arms control were close to the center of policy making during Mr. Kennedy's time as President. And it proved to be a fruitful period, in our home councils and abroad. At home the reassessment of policy started up briskly. Expert knowledge was tapped, new ideas examined, and consultations at a new tempo begun with some of our Western Allies. And within the government that process of consultation—one might even call it negotiation —which precedes major policy developments was put into motion. A general sharpening of concepts followed.

For the first time we sat down to try to figure out exactly how the world might be able to move from its present state of unlimited armament to one of general and complete disarmament, which the United States and other nations had all declared to be their goal. For the first time we worked out and presented, in April 1961, a complete text of a draft nuclear test-ban treaty in all environments. We were thus, within a short time, more certain of the directions in which we wanted to go.

For the first time, also, we worked on actually establishing an independent government agency devoted solely to the study of disarmament questions and the preparation of appropriate legislation. Experience over the years had clearly indicated that the existing situation was not desirable if we were to make progress in this field.[1] There was at the time no important official charged solely with disarmament policy whose voice would be authoritative in the highest councils.

Nor was the personnel situation especially promising: in the State Department the number of officers working in this field had shown a steady decrease, while in the armed services working on disarmament was not regarded as a particularly promising way to open the doors to service advancement and reputation. As a result, we had neither adequate staff for research and policy formulation nor seasoned negotiating teams. This was in contrast with

[1] See Bernard G. Bechhoefer, *Postwar Negotiations for Arms Control* (Washington: The Brookings Institution, 1961), pp. 587-597, for an interesting discussion of the problems, as well as recommendations.

the Soviet Union, which kept large numbers of the same negotiators at the disarmament talks over a period of years.

In 1961 Mr. McCloy was asked to help remedy the situation by drafting a statute for a suitable agency. Together with a number of others, I took part in this effort. In working out the statute, it was our intention to provide a focus within the government for research and policy on disarmament that was independent of other agencies; we wanted the nuclear scientists and seismologists working on disarmament and the test-ban treaty to be removed from the authority of the AEC, and we wanted the military officers assigned to disarmament to take their orders from the disarmament chief and not the Department of Defense or the Joint Chiefs of Staff. We wanted the director of the agency to have easy access to the President and to the Department of State. We felt that the Arms Control and Disarmament Agency (ACDA), which came into being in September 1961, was a good result of our efforts,[2] and since its establishment it has functioned well under the able guidance of William C. Foster, its Director.

On the diplomatic side, we were determined not to be deflected from our efforts, no matter how unreasonable and uncooperative Soviet behavior might seem. We kept on working at what seemed to be the Gordian knot of a nuclear test ban, an effort which was further intensified after the Soviet Union, later in 1961, broke the voluntary moratorium which had been faithfully observed on both sides for almost three years. We thought, studied, and negotiated endlessly on the subject of general disarmament. We also did all we could to clarify for ourselves and for the world the exact, concrete, detailed meaning of the various general Soviet statements and proposals.

Perhaps history will measure the nuclear test-ban treaty of August 5, 1963, as one of the major achievements of President Kennedy's all-too-short term as Chief Executive. It is still too early for any definitive evaluation. Two states which did not sign the treaty, France and Communist China, have since conducted

---

[2] The text of the Act establishing ACDA may be found in United States Arms Control and Disarmament Agency, *Documents on Disarmament, 1961* (Washington: GPO, 1962), pp. 482-495.

nuclear weapons tests in the atmosphere. The ban did, however, serve as a kind of formal punctuation mark, a first step in our efforts for arms control, and it did at least open the way toward further agreement.

Why it is possible to agree at one time and not at another is a tantalizing question. Some would say that friendship or understanding or similarity of ideology are prerequisites, or at least essential lubricants, for international agreement between nations. It is hard to know just what is meant by this: friendship between abstract entities or between national leaders, understanding between individuals or a sharing of ideals? Actually, while it is true that sometimes popular hostility may serve as an obstacle to a particular agreement into which a government may wish to enter, the age-old basis for agreements is not popular sympathy but a nice calculation and balancing of national interests on both sides. A series of pinching crises may lead more readily to agreement than a condition of relaxation.

To a significant degree the urgent Soviet interest in a partial nuclear test-ban treaty in 1963 may be accounted for by a combination of such crises, both domestic and international. Of course, there may be a condition of *détente* in certain aspects of relations between nations and of crisis in other aspects of relations between the same nations. No blanket prescriptions can cover this problem of what conditions are most likely to lead to agreement on a particular subject. The main points to be made are that negotiations with a state basically hostile to us in its ideology can serve a useful and necessary purpose, and that it is worthwhile to pursue such negotiations—intelligently, steadily, and unemotionally—without regard to the political climate of the day. In some ways, useful negotiations among nations are like good health in individuals: the result of a number of factors other than good cheer.

There are two other points worth mentioning before passing on to a more specific discussion of certain aspects of our policies on disarmament and arms control. The first of these is that disarmament and related problems are peculiarly big-power problems; the second is that they are essentially political. There is nothing new about these statements except their special significance given the setting in which they take on practical meaning.

To say that disarmament is peculiarly a big-power problem is to raise at least two intricate questions. First of all, when we are considering general and complete disarmament, we must ask ourselves whether it can be achieved unless all major powers are included in the scheme to be worked out. To put it bluntly, can the United States, Great Britain, and the Soviet Union afford to enter into an agreement if France is not included or if Communist China continues to regard such agreement as irrelevant to its national goals?

The question of French willingness to participate may perhaps be amenable to the passage of time and the hard exigencies of economics. But the matter of the nonparticipation of a Communist China which is in the process of transforming itself into a nuclear power cannot help raising the most serious questions, assuming that the United States and the Soviet Union find themselves able to advance toward the goal of disarmament. Consider for a moment the fact that the United States' Draft Outline of a Treaty on General and Complete Disarmament in a Peaceful World, submitted at Geneva on April 18, 1962, is based on the principle of balance—of a balanced, proportionate, verified reduction of armaments. Is it realistic to pursue such a goal in our negotiations with the Soviet Union while Communist China increases its armaments without check and while a country like North Viet-Nam continues to be armed by both Moscow and Peking? Furthermore, will the Soviet Union not feel less than eager to reduce its armaments with a growing and antagonistic China on its border? Indeed, there are some who feel that Soviet Foreign Minister Andrei Gromyko's proposal in 1962 for a "nuclear umbrella" may have been motivated by a realization of possible danger from the East.

Of course, one should not succumb to hysteria about the immediacy of Communist China's nuclear delivery power, although its technological capacity (illustrated by the tests already made) and its possibilities for political blackmail should not be discounted, as India and countries of Southeast Asia are already aware. Both the United States and the Soviet Union most probably could reduce their armaments considerably in Stage I of any disarmament plan before they ran into any danger from Communist China. Nevertheless, the long-term problem remains. Actually, as far as the United States is concerned, our draft outline disarmament treaty makes it clear that in the drafting process we were well aware of the dangers posed by the nonparticipation of important states when we provided as a condition for the transition from Stage I to Stage II that, among other things, "all militarily significant states had become Parties to the Treaty."[3] The choice is clear though not immediate: either general disarmament including Communist China or no general disarmament.

Saying that disarmament problems are peculiarly great-power problems leads straight into another bramble patch. In any negotiation or detailed "brass-tacks" discussion of disarmament or arms control, what is most important is what the nations possessing the arms say and what in fact they do. The attainment of concrete results will depend on their decisions. This is a plain fact. What the great powers do or do not do, however, will affect millions of people all over the world who do not have significant arms but who do feel a lively concern over, and would be vitally affected by, the consequences of war, especially a nuclear war. Therefore in our era of UN diplomacy disarmament discussions inevitably take place against a background of world scrutiny.

The United Nations is the stage for the presentation of views, discussion, propaganda battles, political maneuver, and on occasion the working out of valuable, though general, blueprints for future consideration. In the General Assembly disarmament problems often become confused with such issues as anticolonialism, bases on foreign soil, nuclear-free zones, and disengagement. The tendency of many of the new nations to include criticism of Western disarmament policies in their general verbal assault on Western actions in Asia or Africa, often while seeking arms for themselves, has hardly advanced the possibilities of constructive negotiation. Nevertheless, the General Assembly, especially when meeting in First Committee, or as the UN Disarmament Commis-

[3] ACDA, *Documents on Disarmament, 1962,* v. I (Washington: GPO, 1963), p. 353.

sion, does offer opportunities for informal exchanges and private conversations, for the quiet development of policies through personal contact. For consideration of a subject such as disarmament, this bringing together of political leaders and diplomats from all over the world in one place can be, potentially, one of the most important functions of the United Nations, even though no agreements are reached.

The situation in the Eighteen-Nation Disarmament Committee in Geneva is somewhat different, more concentrated perhaps, and better suited to negotiation. It is not a UN body, although it has links to the United Nations and submits reports to the General Assembly. As may be remembered, this group, the ENDC, was established in December 1961 by the addition to the existing Ten-Nation Committee of eight new members from the so-called "nonaligned" nations, as the contemporary but not quite accurate term goes.[4] Although the latter eight nations do not distribute their praise or their blame evenly, or even predictably, and although they are not principal negotiating parties, their presence has a certain constructive value. By being there, they serve as a constant and poignant reminder of the interest of the smaller states in disarmament and of their yearning to avoid major war. They also serve to reassure the other nonmember states that their voice is being heard by the great powers. Furthermore, their presence and their vocal interest make it more difficult to break off the discussions. The United States, which has never broken off any disarmament talks, feels that their participation is a good incentive to serious effort. A proposal of some interest may be introduced by an individual member or by the group of eight as a whole. As further valuable services the members of the nonaligned eight at Geneva may seriously consider and work out objective and nonpolitical schemes for regional

[4] Members of the Committee are: Canada, France, Italy, United Kingdom, U.S.A.; Bulgaria, Czechoslovakia, Poland, Rumania, U.S.S.R.; Brazil, Burma, Ethiopia, India, Mexico, Nigeria, Sweden, and U.A.R. The ten members of the original Committee, established in September 1959, are listed first; France refused to participate. Brazil and Mexico, included among the "nonaligned" eight, are members of the Organization of American States. See *U.S. Participation in the U.N.—Report by the President to Congress for the Year 1962* (Washington: GPO, 1963), p. 2.

arms control, make careful and penetrating analyses of the proposals of the great powers, and prod them to greater agreement. But when it comes to the negotiation of texts, this has to be done in small groups by the actual holders of nuclear arms.

The other point indicated above is that disarmament matters are political matters, even though often technical in form. They are intimately related to other vital areas of foreign policy: NATO defense strategy, the balance of power in Asia and the Pacific or in the Western Hemisphere, the German question, and a host of others. They are an integral part of the totality of U.S. relations with the Soviet Union and the Communist world. They should be handled, therefore, by representatives trained in international affairs and acutely aware of the implications of Soviet and Chinese history, ideology, strategy, and tactics. Work and negotiation on disarmament must go forward, whether the political matters have been settled or not, but our proposals and positions must be arrived at and followed up within the total political and military context.

Decisions on policy, moreover, must rest with those whose basic approach and responsibility are political. Because of the awesome nature of modern nuclear weapons, their destructive capacity, their technical intricacy, and the existence of unsolved technical problems, there has been a tendency among the public to accept the scientist's word as final on all aspects of arms and disarmament. And the scientists have felt a responsibility for the results of their work. Called upon to give scientific advice, they have not always been able to keep away from the political or oracular field as well. There can be no doubt that the political negotiator needs the fullest, the best, the latest, and the most objective scientific advice and explanations possible and that he needs these on a continuing objective basis so that he can keep up with the ever-changing scientific scene. Dr. James B. Fisk's work at the Geneva negotiations in 1958 was an admirable example in this respect. The author owes a great debt to his scientific advisers and is very grateful to them. With due respect, this is what the scientist should remain: an adviser on scientific matters to the people who have the training and the responsibility to make political decisions. As Lord Cecil said, "Experts should be on tap but not on top."

It has been my experience in the course of these years of discussion on nuclear weapons and their control that the Western scientist—with his emphasis on the universality of truth and the free exchange of scientific data—often does not concern himself with Soviet political objectives or the arts and wiles of Soviet or Communist negotiating tactics; he sometimes does not sufficiently grasp the fact that his Soviet counterpart has a directed role to play in a politically determined and far-reaching strategy.

As Sir Eric Ashby, the Master of Clare College, Cambridge, has put it, the Western scientist remains united to other scientists not only by common beliefs in the science in which both are experts, "but by a willingness to accept on trust the common beliefs of other scientists in fields outside [his] own expert knowledge."[5] Eager to "get the job done," often unaware or scornful of the political implications of technical Soviet proposals, confident, on occasion, that the scientific mind can solve the political and constitutional problems which have long fazed nonscientists, the Western scientist sometimes accepts at face value Soviet proposals which he cannot really judge on his own and the political significance of which he does not fully grasp.

One such example was the Pugwash Statement on nuclear test detection of September 1962, in which the concept of automated "black boxes" for the recording of seismic data was accepted by Western scientists who were not seismologists and who therefore had no real basis for any authoritative judgment as to the value of such instruments.[6] Furthermore, the scientists also accepted the proposal of Soviet scientists that on-site inspections under the proposed nuclear test-ban control treaty would not be mandatory but would be "considered" by a country after a "request" by the international control commission, a proposal which would render almost meaningless the entire concept of impartial on-site inspection in order to identify otherwise unidentified seismic events.

[5] "A University Presidency: What It Takes," *Saturday Review*, November 21, 1964, p. 78.
[6] Pugwash Statement on Test Detection, as reproduced in *Bulletin of the Atomic Scientists*, November 1962, p 41. (See also Cmd. 1958, *Miscellaneous No. 5, Further Documents Relating to the Conference of the 18-Nation Committee on Disarmament* [London: H.M.S.O., 1963], pp. 66-67.) It was signed by three Soviet scientists and by D. R. Inglis, A. Rich, and R. S. Leghorn of the United States.

No one can deny that the advance of science has made possible the powerful weapons of today and that science itself must have a great role if we are to succeed in controlling such weapons. But when it comes to how to proceed in establishing that control, the political or governmental objective should determine the scientific program, not the other way around. We need the help of the scientists in considering what can and cannot be done through scientific means. Even there, however, scientists have sometimes been in error in the past; some have done what others deemed unlikely or impossible. The able and brilliant Vannevar Bush, writing in 1949, recorded his vote against "high-trajectory guided missiles . . . spanning thousands of miles and precisely hitting chosen targets," and did so for a number of plausible reasons since proved untrue.[7] Dr. Edward Teller went ahead on the H-bomb even though many said it could not be done. Science in this field is too much in a state of flux and discovery for anyone to be certain that some things can or cannot be done until a good deal of effort has been devoted to examining specific problems. One has only to think of the vast changes in the last few years in nuclear weapons, in seismological knowledge, in missiles, in verification systems, in space research and technology. That is why the political goal should be set by those with political responsibility. Then every effort should be made to supply the scientific instruments and the monetary support for scientific research necessary to reach that goal.

We should also examine quite closely the education we give our scientists in order to bolster their understanding of the society in which they live and of the world conditions in which decisions vital to our country's future must be made. As one recent study put it, "Perhaps . . . the newly emerging generation of scientists [should] be required to serve a kind of postgraduate internship on the relation of science to society. . . ."[8] Although some institutions of higher learning have started on such an effort, it needs to be enlarged. At the same time we should deter-

[7] *Modern Arms and Free Men* (New York: Simon and Schuster, 1949), pp. 84-86.

[8] Ralph E. Lapp, *The New Priesthood, the Scientific Elite and the Uses of Power* (New York: Harper & Row, 1965), p. 229.

mine where we need to strengthen our scientific training. We should always be scanning our scientific progress in relation to the political needs of the present and the future and not be circumscribed in our vision. Thus, for example, if it is technically feasible to develop verification procedures which would make on-site inspection for otherwise unidentified underground explosions unnecessary or marginal, then research for such a program, the underground Vela project for example, should not be hampered by lack of money or, perhaps more important, of personnel or scientific information.

*   *   *

With these introductory remarks, which should provide some idea of the author's viewpoint, or his bias, let us turn to the body of the book. Too brief to be a history, too dry to be a memoir, it is in the nature of a personal disquisition on certain topics of particular importance to America's future. The value of negotiating with the Russians, their diplomatic style, certain aspects of the search for general disarmament, possible limited measures of arms control, the nuclear test ban, the critical problems of verification and enforcement—these topics are treated on the basis of personal experience and the author's own thought and analysis.

The concluding section will deal with what I consider the overriding arms problem of our time: the prevention of the further proliferation of nuclear weapons. A formidable, unparalled task which will require unprecedented decisions and sacrifices on the part of a number of nations, it must be accomplished soon or not at all. The draft treaty submitted by the United States at Geneva on August 17, 1965, poses the problem, but there is still far to go, and in very limited time.

Chapter II

Disarmament Diplomacy

The value of the disarmament talks in Geneva and elsewhere is bound to be questioned, if only for the reason that they have gone on so long and produced so little. It has been obscured, also, by the agitated international climate in which they take place. Thus, my good friend, David E. Lilienthal, in his book, *Change, Hope, and the Bomb,* can argue that even discussing nuclear disarmament on the diplomatic level adds so directly to international hostility and tension that it should be stopped and attention turned instead to supposedly less agitating topics in the social, economic, and cultural fields.[1]

This argument seems not merely overpessimistic but unreal. In fact, disarmament talks in themselves have not changed the international temperature one way or the other. And even the opposite is not always true, for disarmament talks have sometimes continued in the midst of resounding crisis. This point has been illustrated recently by the holding of disarmament sessions in Geneva while the fighting in Viet-Nam grew in intensity. Furthermore, there is no reason why disarmament and other topics cannot simultaneously be under discussion or negotiation, as indeed they often have been. Perhaps it is the tone of the discussions, particularly the Soviet statements, as reported in the press that shocks people and leads to a conclusion that the meetings themselves generate hostility. Daily press reporting often overlooks useful, constructive, and nonpolemical statements

[1] Princeton University Press, 1963, Ch. IV.

which are not "news." The use of rough, impolite, and even vituperative language by Soviet representatives is a diplomatic style which Communists have affected in greater or less degree from the days of the Revolution of 1917, in order to show their contempt for capitalism and for "imperialistic warmongers." It has become stereotyped. It is much like the traffic noise that assails our ears in so many places today: it may be annoying but does not prevent one's getting ahead with the business at hand.

Others deny the value of the talks in Geneva and at the United Nations because they have not resulted in negotiated agreements, apart from the partial test-ban treaty, the so-called "hot-line" agreement, and the agreement not to place nuclear weapons in vehicles orbiting in outer space. This is perhaps a more interesting criticism, as it raises the question of how one measures the success or failure of a diplomatic negotiation or conference, especially one so long extended in time as the discussions on disarmament. In considering the purposes of both sides, one has to weigh the results of negotiating, with or without agreement, against those of not negotiating at all.

There have, of course, been times at Geneva when we have engaged in a real negotiating process, giving that term its traditional definition of an attempt to settle international differences through an orderly bargaining procedure intended to result in a mutually beneficial written agreement. This was the case in the working out of the Resolution on War Propaganda in May 1962.

There were also other times when we, on the Western side, were engaged honestly and conscientiously in a negotiating process but sensed that the other side was not. This was true in much of the discussion we had on the nuclear test-ban treaty prior to March 1961, when the reintroduction of the proposal to establish the international executive organ on a "troika" basis, complete with veto power, showed us clearly that the Soviet Union did not mean business at least not currently.

The truth is that it takes at least two to carry through a serious negotiation to the point of an agreement. Much of the time during the many years devoted to discussion on disarmament— though not all of the time—the Soviet Union was not interested in that kind of negotiation but merely in giving the appearance of it, thus reaping propaganda benefits while going ahead with its own arms programs and shielding itself from any intrusion. This conclusion is clear from the "stalling" tactics of Soviet representatives, from the lack of real content in their disarmament proposals, from their inexhaustible fund of objections to our proposals, and from the lack of response to the concessions made to their point of view. For example, in the long exchanges during the nuclear test-ban talks of 1961 and 1962 on instituting inspections to check up on otherwise unidentified seismic events, the closer we came to their position on this subject by limiting the area, method, and number of on-site inspections, the more determined the Soviet representatives seemed to become in their rejections.

In the field of general disarmament we face deep differences of outlook and goals. Therefore it is our duty while pushing forward to "go slow," in the sense of agreeing only to sufficiently precise and careful proposals. Fortunately, the United States has been able successfully to resist pressures from various nations to enter into vague and high-sounding agreements on general disarmament in circumstances which could lead only to increased tensions and dangers to international security.

Furthermore, we are also dealing with a subject which is still relatively so unexplored that it is important not to enter into any agreements which might make it difficult to adjust to the results of new discoveries and new knowledge. This caveat does not apply in the same degree to the more precise measures of arms control and limited disarmament which have been under discussion from time to time.

The Reasons for Negotiation

If, then, we should not judge the disarmament talks by the number of negotiated and ratified agreements they have produced, how should we judge them? Why, in other words, does the U.S. government continue to have its representatives sit through hours and days of apparently unproductive meetings, exposed to repetitious and often insulting attacks by Soviet representatives? The answer is simple: although we cannot be certain that continued discussions will have a positive result, we are convinced that disrupting them would set back our search for a more peaceful and more stable world.[2] Therefore we have made, and should continue to make, every effort to keep the talks going. This maxim applies even when Soviet action disrupts them, as was the case in 1960, and 1961, and again in 1965.

In general, we have regarded time as a possible ally. On the political front, though we did not in 1961 anticipate any basic changes in Soviet policy, we did think that the Soviet Union was confronted with a wide variety of problems which might lead to some re-evaluation of its immediate international goals and possibly also to a more accommodating policy at Geneva. Among them were relations with Communist China and with the increasingly vocal and independent East European satellites, domestic pressures for a reallocation of resources to the production of consumer goods, and reassessment of military needs caused by technological change. We wanted to give Soviet thinking on all these problems time to ripen in the hope that there would be a favorable impact on the course of disarmament talks—on both sides of the table.

We also saw the value of time in relation to scientific change. We realized very clearly that in having to deal with constantly developing nuclear weapons, ballistic missiles, computers, long-range photography, arrays of seismograph clusters in deep holes, the vigorous expansion of the Vela research and space programs, and such matters, we were entering a field which scientific knowledge was only beginning to penetrate. Progress in the Vela program of nuclear detection satellites inevitably will change the picture as we saw it during past negotiations.[3]

---

[2] Arthur H. Dean, in *Department of State Bulletin,* January 28, 1963, p. 123.

[3] The first of the advanced Vela nuclear detection satellites are scheduled to be launched in pairs by a Titan III-C rocket at Cape Kennedy, Florida, in 1966. With these second-generation Vela satellites and the three pairs of first-generation Velas now orbiting the earth some 55,000 miles out, the prospect of anyone being able to run a sneak nuclear blast anywhere in the air, atmosphere, or space of the solar system becomes improbable. But thus far the proposed advanced Velas, as well as those now in operation, detect only high-altitude blasts and, so far as is known, would not detect an underground explosion unless radioactivity were to be vented in the air.

In fact, everyone at first shared a vast ignorance concerning the actual conditions under which disarmament could take place with safety for all. We therefore saw that the scientific position of today might not be wholly relevant for tomorrow and that by keeping the talks going we might be giving ourselves a chance to make new, more acceptable suggestions, always consonant with the needs of our national security and without losing sight of the ultimately hostile and revolutionary nature of Soviet goals. It was a combination of a process of scientific change and political re-evaluation on our side, and a patent willingness to study Soviet proposals objectively, that made possible our new suggestions in August 1962 for a partial nuclear test ban. With relatively few changes, these suggestions formed the basis for the partial nuclear test-ban treaty signed in Moscow on August 5, 1963.

These were background considerations arguing for patience and persistence in keeping the talks on disarmament going. More in the foreground were certain specific goals for which we felt the continuing talks to be especially suited. These goals concerned education, clarification, and preparation.

The discussions—at Geneva, at the United Nations, and in confidential diplomatic conversations—were a necessary means whereby the nations of the world could become educated on disarmament questions and the ground could be broken for concrete agreements. This was a continuing process carried on in a

---

The first Vela detection satellites were sent aloft in October 1963, the second pair went in July 1964, and the third pair went in July 1965. Each in a pair of Vela detection satellites was put into an identical circular orbit but covering opposite sides of the earth. They are studded externally with twelve X-ray detectors and inside carry six gamma and one neutron detector, which can spot rays from a one-megaton nuclear explosion millions of miles beyond the range of earth-bound devices. There has been no difficulty in putting any of the Velas into orbit, and all three sets are sending satisfactory reports back to the earth.

Both versions of Velas have what are called "logic boxes," which are supposed to be able to distinguish between nuclear explosions and "false alarms" caused by cosmic showers, solar plasma, and natural background radiation. Thus far the Velas have not detected anything that could be considered a sneak Soviet nuclear space blast, but they have detected gamma rays from as far off as Mars, Venus, and the sun. These Vela detection satellites are launched into a high orbit of 55,000 miles to avoid the Van Allen belt, a pulsating belt of radiation that extends from 450 miles to 40,000 miles into space.

comparatively normal, diplomatic manner and with an avoidance of crisis. No hurriedly summoned *ad hoc* or summit conference, meeting for a limited time, and high expectations amid great publicity, could have duplicated the work that was accomplished in this way.

It is a fact that very few nations in the world are in a position to carry out the necessary research and analytic thinking on disarmament matters. The United States is the center of such endeavors. There is much interesting thinking going on also in Great Britain. This is not to ignore the stimulating ideas that emerge from other countries. But too many statesmen, with an eye on the Nobel Peace Prize, come forward with proposals that hit the front page but are both unrealistic and dangerous. As far as we could tell from the materials presented by Soviet representatives and from other sources of information, there was very little basic research on disarmament in the Soviet Union, or at least nothing comparable to the scale of the objective effort being conducted in the United States and Great Britain.

We felt it therefore to be our particular responsibility to make as certain as we could that other nations were aware of the scientific facts involved in disarmament problems, so that they could both understand the bases for our policies and be better informed in the formulation of their own. We could not gauge accurately what the Soviet reactions were, because Soviet representatives school themselves so carefully not to react, except officially, and because we know so little about the secretive process which is Soviet policy making. Our working papers and our statements in the verbatim records were available and did go to Moscow. Unfortunately for the possibility of careful true dialogue, there was no willingless on the part of the Soviet government to share freely with the world the results of its research on the scientific basis for its policies.

We do know, however, that the non-Communist smaller nations, especially those which participate in the ENDC at Geneva and have neither the personnel nor the finances to devote to basic research on disarmament, considered it valuable and informative to be exposed to the results of our thinking and to our painstaking and precise answers to their questions. Of course, other channels of information are open; one should not exag-

gerate the impact of such diplomatic conferences. But they are
unique because they are "live."

The existence of the talks, moreover, greatly spurred the research on disarmament undertaken in the United States. Since
there was a forum, programs had to be prepared for it and the
proposals of others considered. Furthermore, if the United States
was to keep its leadership in the field and prevent others from
running wild with propositions far removed from the actual
issues, its own representatives had to be well prepared and to
know their own position clearly. All this required intensive research and thinking. Moreover, these lengthy negotiations provided our diplomats with an intimate and firsthand acquaintance
with Soviet negotiating methods, tactics, and ways of thinking,
an experience valuable beyond the limits of these often repetitious and (apart from the three limited agreements that have
been reached) apparently unproductive discussions.

In addition to the opportunities for the sharing of information
which arose at the talks, there was the possibility for the clarification and exposure of policies. For one thing, we ourselves came to
see our image more clearly after seeing how it was reflected in the
minds of others. For example, in early 1961 John J. McCloy and
I were impressed by the fact that although the United States was
not against complete and general disarmament, many nations
seemed to believe that it was.[4] Furthermore, by not taking an
unequivocal position in favor of general and complete disarmament, and indeed by not stating clearly or even knowing exactly
what our position was, we were dissipating our leadership; there
was the danger of the field being dominated altogether too much
by nations which were aware neither of the problems involved
nor of the responsibilities of power, or by individuals willing to
sacrifice national interest for personal fame, or by fanatics or
moralists to whom national interest meant nothing.

Since, to our minds, the argument with the Soviet Union on
the terms "general and complete disarmament" or "arms control" was largely one of semantics, in that the terms were not
sharply distinguished by translation into Russian, we suggested
to Washington that the United States put forward a proposal for

[4] See also Bernhard G. Bechhoefer, *Postwar Negotiations for Arms Control* (Washington: The Brookings Institution, 1961), p. 439.

general and complete disarmament. Though hardly a practical proposition for negotiating under existing conditions, it would evince our own deep interest in ending the arms race and in reducing tensions. It would also cut down the propaganda returns which the Soviet Union was at that time reaping from its declared position as an advocate of general and complete disarmament, while we appeared in the role of a reluctant suitor or captious quibbler in favor only of "arms control" or "arms reduction" or "limitation." Presient Kennedy and various other high officials of the government approved of the idea, although objections were raised by members of the Joint Chiefs of Staff, whose statutory and professional obligation it is to safeguard our military position as they see it.[5]

As a result, for the first nine months or so of 1961 the U.S. government, in all its relevant departments and agencies and at the highest level, was engaged in an unprecedented stocktaking effort to find out in detail just what sort of a military establishment the United States required for the protection of itself and its allies. What types of disarmament and arms control measures could we afford; how could we safely move through successive stages from the present situation of massive armament to a condition of total disarmament; and, in the increasing absence of arms, what new institutions for keeping the peace and for settling conflicts would be required? Some of these questions were in pioneer territory and we succeeded only in mapping their main features. Finally, after a number of hardheaded, detailed, frank, and closely reasoned discussions, in which President Kennedy took a keen personal interest, we were able to agree on a draft declaration to serve "as a guide for the negotiation of a program for general and complete disarmament in a peaceful world," which, it was intended, the President would make known before the UN General Assembly in September 1961.[6]

To digress briefly to the matter of the domestic handling of

[5] The duties of the Joint Chiefs of Staff are summarized in the *United States Government Organization Manual, 1965-66* (Washington: GPO, 1965), pp. 141-142.

[6] Richard P. Stebbins, ed., *Documents on American Foreign Relations, 1961* (New York: Harper & Row, for the Council on Foreign Relations, 1962), pp. 221-228 for the U.S. declaration; and pp. 473-485 for President Kennedy's address.

policy, at this point in early September 1961 President Kennedy came under a heavy cross fire of interests and advice. On the one hand there were arguments that the Berlin crisis would require our rearmament and that this was therefore not the time to talk of disarming. Other protests came from politically powerful representatives of states with defense industries, especially California and Texas, who feared any disarmament measure which might have a deleterious effect on the economies of their states. There were also those on the President's personal staff, with a fierce personal loyalty to him, who felt that sponsoring any measure which might run counter to the President's election promise to keep the economy going on a high level should be postponed. Mr. McCloy and I were both Republicans serving the President in a nonpartisan capacity because of our views as to the great importance of controlling the arms race.

The President's difficulties came to my attention when Theodore Sorensen telephoned me on September 18, 1961, to say that the President was being counseled not to make his disarmament speech, on which Mr. McCloy and I had worked, to the UN General Assembly on September 25. Distressed by this information, I sent a telegram to Mr. Kennedy at Hyannisport, urging him to view disarmament in the long-term perspective and pointing out that there had been those who had counseled President Lincoln against issuing the Emancipation Proclamation during the Civil War. On Monday, the 21st, the President came to the Hotel Carlyle in New York. Throughout the day there was much discussion, which he finally resolved by deciding to make the speech putting the United States on record for general and complete disarmament in a peaceful world. President Kennedy was a man firmly anchored in reality, but he had the rare quality of not allowing the reality of a particular moment to paralyze his capacity to take bold, imaginative, and courageous steps.

Clarification of policy was not confined to a sharpening of our own positions and proposals; it also included the exposure of the veiled positions of others. Our effort was concentrated on moving the talks, both on general disarmament and on the test ban, away from propaganda and vague schemes directed to temporary political advantage toward a precise consideration of the military,

political, economic, and scientific problems actually involved and
to a sober view of their implications. In so doing, we exposed the
Soviet program for general and complete disarmament for what
it was: a plan for achieving Soviet strategic-military dominance
and hence for the ultimate political victory of the Soviet Union
over the rest of the world.[7]

In exposing it, at Geneva and New York, we asked detailed,
pointed questions of the Soviet representatives; we made precise
proposals; we made specific amendments to our own proposals;
we sought to take account of the views of the "nonaligned" as far
as we reasonably and safely could; and we asked the Soviet representatives to supply scientific and military evidence in support of
their positions, which we knew to be scientifically and militarily
untenable. In response to all our efforts, the Soviet representatives were unable to produce anything more than general accusations, vague and unanchored statements, and blank refusals to
consider the implications of the steps they proposed. Gradually it
became clear for all to see that the Soviets were on the defensive
and that their Draft Treaty on General and Complete Disarmament, submitted on March 15, 1962, though showy to start with,
when unwrapped under our persistent questioning, was actually
full of gaps, traps, and tawdry tinsel.

In addition to this purpose of unmasking (to use a favorite
Soviet term), it was also our intention to make it more difficult
for the Soviet government to continue to take refuge in sweeping
general statements while avoiding precision and actual commitment. In this double effort we met with considerable success. The
statement on inspection accompanying the Joint Statement of
Agreed Principles of September 1961 and the text of the War
Propaganda Resolution of May 1962 are relevant examples.

The Incident of the War Propaganda Resolution

On the question of war propaganda we had a familiar situation. For quite some time the Soviet Union had been suggesting
that we work out a joint statement outlawing war propaganda.

[7] Dean, cited, p. 122.

The Soviets were making "hay" with the "nonaligned" or new nations out of our refusal to ban "war propaganda." Although our refusal was based on the constitutional grounds of the separation of powers in the United States between federal and state governments and on the protection of freedom of speech under the First Amendment, as well as on our difficulty with such an inherently vague concept as outlawing "war propaganda," it seemed to me that it was not fitting for a democratic government such as ours, with its concern for peace, to continue to take a negative attitude and that we should make a strong effort to see if something acceptable could be negotiated.

Permission from Washington was granted, though the general opinion was that the effort was hopeless. Talks began between Valerian A. Zorin, Deputy Foreign Minister and then head of the Soviet delegation, and myself at the U.S. delegation's office in Geneva one Saturday morning at nine o'clock. They went on around the clock that weekend and at various other times, orthodox and unorthodox, for four weeks. Irregular, long, and Sunday hours are part of the diplomat's fare. Where there is a desire to negotiate, no one should think of the position of the hands on the clock or the day of the week.

It was an interesting experience in a number of ways. Both the urgency given to it by the Soviet delegation and the effort on Ambassador Zorin's part to understand the American position were quite refreshing. The discussion started from two acutely different points of view. The original Soviet draft revealed again the Soviet concentration on the government's complete powers as against the individual; thus it contained provisions for the widest obligations on the part of governments to suppress war propaganda, broadly defined to include appeals for preventive nuclear war and for revision of frontiers resulting from World War II, as well as to outlaw calls for the use of force against peoples which have embarked "on the course of national liberation." Support for wars of "national liberation" was included in the official definition of the Soviet policy of peaceful coexistence.

The Soviet proposal also would have obliged signatory states to ensure the passage of legislation declaring war propaganda in any form "a grave crime against peace and humanity" and providing severe penalties for persons guilty of such propaganda. Such broad provisions, penalties, and limitations on the individual were not acceptable to us because they were in conflict with our constitutional system, which allows people broad latitude to express all sorts of currently unpopular views as long as no incitement to disorder is involved.

In explaining the situation to Ambassador Zorin, I found even this high-ranking Soviet official basically unaware of the way in which our federal governmental system operates under a written constitution giving it limited powers, and with a Bill of Rights for its citizens. The inability of the U.S. government to order its citizens not to criticize the Soviet Union seemed to him at first no more than a joke and not to be taken seriously. After detailed and patient explanations, however, and by dint of careful drafting and redrafting, we were finally able to work out a text which protected the U.S. government under its Constitution and which was also acceptable to him. Thus, to take only one example, the blanket obligation for punitive legislation contained in the original Soviet draft was changed to a call on all states to adopt, "within the limits of their constitutional systems, appropriate measures . . . to give effect to the declaration." Also, the emphasis was shifted from a negative concentration on prohibiting war propaganda to a positive emphasis on the widest possible circulation of "news, ideas and opinions" conducive to the strengthening of peace and friendship among peoples and to the extension of cultural, scientific, and educational relations among them.[8]

Ambassador Zorin seemed well pleased with the final result and so expressed himself. He may have felt that he had been able to nail the United States down in a resolution which he too, perhaps, had despaired of ever being able to achieve. Indeed, when he announced our agreement at Geneva in the ENDC's Committee of the Whole, whose proceedings are not binding until formal action is taken in a subsequent plenary session, he stated that this wonderful step was thoroughly acceptable to his government and that he would support it fully at the next

[8] United States Arms Control and Disarmament Agency, *Documents on Disarmament, 1962*, v. I (Washington: GPO, 1963), pp. 545-552.

plenary session. We accepted it too as a constructive way of eliminating an old chestnut long on the agenda, and the discussion ended amid general jubilation on the part of "nonaligned" representatives at the encouraging "tone" which the conference had taken.

Then an interesting epilogue took place. After a few days of fulsome praise of the resolution, the Soviet radio suddenly began to criticize it, and it was apparent that Ambassador Zorin had turned out to be the loser in the battle of opposing Soviet viewpoints that we assume is always going on within the higher governmental circles in the Kremlin, but of which we get very few actual examples. At the next plenary session of the ENDC the Bulgarian delegate, who was sometimes given what one might call the "axing" jobs, began to criticize the resolution. And then Ambassador Zorin actually tried to expunge from the official record all of his favorable references to the War Propaganda Resolution, thus trying to create the impression that the U.S.S.R. had never agreed to the document.

This revealing effort, which was not successful, made a deep impression on a number of the "nonaligned" delegates. Indeed, the entire episode is instructive, especially to those who insist that all disarmament disagreements are caused by the "negative-minded" and recalcitrant American representatives.

The Joint Statement of Agreed Principles

Another important example of discussions as an instrument for clarifying Soviet aims and policies is to be found in the proceedings surrounding the Joint Statement of Agreed Principles for Disarmament Negotiations, agreed on by the United States and the Soviet Union and submitted to the General Assembly on September 20, 1961. In March of that year, Moscow and Washington had agreed that private talks be started between their representatives in the hope of finding some formula by which the disarmament talks, broken off by the Soviet walkout from the Ten-Nation Disarmament Conference in June 1960, could be reconvened. Actually, the U.S.S.R. wanted bilateral Soviet-American negotiations on the substance of disarmament issues, but we felt that these crucial issues had to be worked out in a forum much larger than bilateral meetings. We hit on the device of a Joint Statement of Agreed Principles as the basis for later multilateral talks, and, in any case, we did not think it likely that anything more than such a statement could be achieved at that time. In this we were indeed right, since the working out of the statement was in itself a major task. Mr. McCloy conducted the talks successively in Washington, Moscow, and New York, as Special Representative of the President, with the author alternating as necessary when Mr. McCloy was not present.

Careful, painstaking, exploratory discussions went on for some five months, with gradually accumulating agreements right up to the very day the statement was made public. At the start we were faced with a brief, skeletal document from the Soviet government, demanding unquestioning support for the principle of general and complete disarmament on a "take it or leave it" basis. As Ambassador Zorin put it, we could accept the document or he would "go home." Mr. McCloy, however, has an unusual ability to combine firmness with a scholarly zeal for exploring the attitudes and concerns of the other side. Methodically and patiently he was able to continue the talks and to expand their scope to include a number of principles that were important to us. However, as time went on, it became clear that, like the Scriptures, the principles could be given varying interpretations.

It was a demanding process. Day by day there would be conferences with the Soviet representatives. In the evenings and on weekends our team would meet to work out our own responses and to interpret the Soviet position. It was also a slow process, since we had to work out our policy position with the participation of many departments and agencies of our own government in a kind of internal negotiation within a foreign negotiation. The Soviet responses were also slow, as they were probably going through a similar process on their side. We had the impression, unsubstantiated but nevertheless strong, that Premier Khrushchev wanted the talks continued to a successful conclusion.

This particular stage in the whole course of discussions on disarmament deserves to be emphasized for two reasons. First of all, during the exchange we began to have a feeling that it might at last be possible to have reasonable negotiations with Soviet representatives on the subject of arms control and disarmament. In this sense it was a kind of a turning point even though the hope was often to be disappointed. In addition, it was during these talks that we were able to achieve an important clarification of the Soviet position on the issue of inspection.

The clarification came about in the following way. Mr. Mc-Cloy and I had carefully pored over all Soviet statements made on the subject of inspection in 1959 and 1960. They used sweeping language. But what the statements amounted to was agreement to inspect weapons brought to depots for destruction and nothing more; in other words, there was no permission to look in the closets or in the cupboards or under the rugs to see whether anything had been overlooked or concealed. Having had bitter experience with inadequate inspection in postarmistice operations in Korea and being generally aware of the pitfalls of such a position, we were unable to accept it as a basis for a joint statement and continued to insist on inspection of retained armaments as well as those to be destroyed. As our talks proceeded, the matter of inspection remained the only major point of dissension. Ambassador Zorin stated flatly that, while full inspection *after* general and complete disarmament would be acceptable, inspection and verification of existing armaments and facilities *before* then would be espionage, and that he could not continue the talks on this basis.

We then drafted an article defining inspection as covering both stocks to be destroyed and those retained. Taking account of Ambassador Zorin's position that this definition would not be acceptable in the joint statement, we asked whether he would accept the rest of the statement and not object to the dispatch of a public letter to the missions of all United Nations members, giving full information on the differences over inspection and specifically reserving the right to bring up the topic again. Actually, of course, the idea of such a letter was quite objectionable to Ambassador Zorin, as it destroyed the possibility of a "waiving" gambit in this particular episode. It is a favorite device of Soviet diplomats to press the adversary to set aside some aspect of a question in the interests of getting agreement and of moving ahead and then, when the other party brings up the matter later, to claim that by agreeing to set it aside originally the other party had agreed to waive it entirely. We were familiar with this approach and determined to make it crystal clear that nothing had been "waived." The agreement on the statement, without the clause in question, was made public, as was a letter from Mr. McCloy to Ambassador Zorin making our position on inspection absolutely clear.[9] The letter was distributed to all delegations to the General Assembly, regardless of the feeling of some that it was a "tactless" move.

Looking back at this experience of discussion, tough bargaining, and patient drafting and redrafting, one can with justice conclude that we were able to achieve as much agreement as was possible at the time. We made explicit some of the theretofore fuzzy content of the term "general and complete disarmament" and put ourselves into a much better position for any subsequent negotiations on a substantive disarmament treaty. In addition, by achieving this agreement, we removed one roadblock in the way of renewed discussion of disarmament at Geneva. We had also made it very clear to everyone just how limited the Soviet concept of inspection was. As Mr. McCloy put it later, his exchange of letters with Ambassador Zorin had for the first time brought into the open "the essential difference between the Soviet and Allied concepts of inspection and control."[10] Now everyone could see the difference and draw his own conclusions.

Finally, the whole course of diplomatic exchange over this period offered an opportunity for a valuable clearing up of misunderstanding and obfuscation as a preparation for possible agreement. We were always on the lookout for such an opportunity. The partial test-ban treaty of August 1963 probably would not have been concluded when and as it was in Moscow in July 1963 without the patient, intensive, preparatory clarifications and exchanges and amendments which had taken place at Geneva through 1961 and 1962. That effort, even with all its discouragements and limited results, represents the most fruitful period of our disarmament negotiations to date.

---

[9] Stebbins, *Documents on American Foreign Relations, 1961,* cited, pp. 200-204.
[10] "Balance Sheet on Disarmament," *Foreign Affairs,* April 1962, p. 358.

The Soviet Style

Diplomatic style is a kind of national signature, reflecting not only official policies but also characteristics of the society from which the diplomat comes and the outlook in which he has been bred. It influences heavily the reactions of a particular diplomat and the procedures he will be likely to follow. Knowing intimately the diplomatic style of one's adversary, besides being in itself fascinating, can be a real negotiating advantage.

In considering Soviet diplomacy as a whole, two major characteristics stand out: a dogmatic expectation of hostility from the outside world and an iron determination to carry out a program previously determined in Moscow and not subject to change by the diplomat in the field.

The expectation of hostility, which arises from Communist theory and is reinforced by a selective reading of history, permeates every aspect of official Soviet diplomatic behavior. Every Western proposal on disarmament was examined meticulously by the Soviet representatives with a view to discovering its "real, nefarious purpose." Ideological warfare was expected from us, just as it was being conducted by them. In other words, the Soviet diplomat often seemed to think of himself as a "traveler by night in the forest who must be constantly on the watch for the smallest sound or sight of treachery."[11] As a result, his official stance at the conference table was rigid, often rude or at least barely polite, secretive, formal, very general, and given to diatribes and not dialogue as the safest way of dealing with almost any question. As I listened expectantly to innumerable Soviet statements, it seemed to me that both in substance and in form they concealed a curious mixture of feelings of arrogance and fear.

The result has been an inflexibility which marks both Soviet policy itself and the conduct of the diplomats charged with communicating it.[12] That the Soviet diplomat is determined to stand by his fixed position and that he lacks discretionary powers is certainly not news. One result is, of course, that he must wait

[11] Philip E. Mosely, "Some Soviet Techniques of Negotiation," in *Negotiating with the Russians,* ed. by Raymond Dennett and Joseph E. Johnson (Boston: World Peace Foundation, 1951), p. 296.

[12] Compare James Reston's interview with Soviet Premier Aleksei Kosygin, published in *The New York Times* on December 8, 1965.

for instructions—though rarely admitting it—before he can react to a new proposal, however logical, or suggest changes. He may, therefore, conduct "stalling" or "long-talking" tactics which may slow up the proceedings for weeks or months.

The Western diplomat, having started his schooling some years ago, is by now accustomed and impervious to the gritty official Soviet style. Indeed, given the vast differences in purposes between Moscow and the West, negotiation was bound to be a difficult and tedious process under any circumstances. This was particularly true when the subject was disarmament, directly affecting the world's military balance, at a time when none of the major political conflicts had been settled. A more flexible and unpolemical public manner on the part of Soviet representatives might have made the procedure more pleasant and perhaps less time-consuming, though without guaranteeing better results. But then, perhaps, it is impossible to think of oneself as a revolutionary and be polite to "capitalist reactionaries" as well. Quite possibly, the Soviet Union might have done better in political terms had its diplomats tried to do some serious selling of Soviet points.

There are some variations, however. The style of the Soviet diplomat reveals an interesting dichotomy. In formal sessions attended by large delegations and sometimes also by the press he presents what has come to be the traditional stern face of Soviet diplomacy, with polemics and denunciation his main tools and a scoring of propaganda points his main objective; but in private, off-the-record meetings—such as the daily ones of the co-chairmen at Geneva—he can be cordial and much more reasonable. On such occasions it was possible for my Soviet opposite number and myself to talk dispassionately and intelligently about a number of controversial topics, to explore each other's meanings and interpretations, and to get down to detailed drafting. These private working sessions were a welcome relief from the time-consuming, repetitious, and by then rather banal, long-winded, and stereotyped exchanges at the official sessions. In short, experience suggests that the Soviet government assigns different functions to the two different types of meetings where the audiences differ.

We welcomed the tone of these informal discussions, although we also realized that pleasant conversations and real communication are not necessarily synonymous. We had no direct way of knowing what influence these sessions might have on Soviet policy and thinking, but proceeded on the assumption that any opportunity for the calm, uninterrupted explanation of our position on a continuing basis was better than none. We also wanted to hear the Soviet point of view in a setting free of polemics.

Informal Meetings of the Co-chairmen

At the test-ban negotiations in Geneva in 1961, attended only by the Soviet Union, the United States, and Great Britain, there had been opportunities for informal conferences. But, oddly enough, though he did not intend it, we have Krishna Menon, then Defense Minister and delegate of India, to thank for setting in motion the events that led to the start of the private exchanges in the spring of 1962. The Eighteen-Nation Disarmament Conference had just started and had taken over the earlier test-ban conference by the device of creating a tripartite (U.S., U.K., and Soviet) ENDC subcommittee, which met separately, to consider that problem. It was the Indian representative who insisted that, in addition to the plenary meetings of the ENDC and the Test-Ban Subcommittee, there should be informal meetings to which any member of the ENDC might come to discuss whatever aspect of relevant problems he wished, without agenda and without an official record. As a result of this initiative, informal meetings of the Committee of the Whole began on March 19, 1962.

As we had anticipated, the "unstructured" meetings, where prepared statements were not supposed to be presented, started off with the reading by the Communist representatives of lengthy prepared statements, of which they had a record and we did not. Three meetings were wasted in this manner, and the whole idea of informal meetings fell into disrepute. They were called only infrequently thereafter. However, the need for informal discussion was still apparent. Here again an Indian representative, this time Arthur Lall, had been laying the groundwork. He had been pushing the idea of bilateral contacts between the two co-chairmen because he had seen them proved effective at the Geneva Conference on Laos (then nearing its end); and there had been many bilateral talks at the test-ban negotiations with the approval of our British allies. I then proposed to Ambassador Zorin, with the complete agreement of my Western colleagues, the expediency of informal meetings with him alone, and he agreed. The conference officially blessed this arrangement and gave the co-chairmen formal status and responsibilities.

Our co-chairmen meetings usually took place toward the end of the afternoon, after the plenary sessions on disarmament and after the tripartite sessions on the test ban, and sometimes lasted for several hours. No notes were taken, no stenographers were present; the atmosphere was workmanlike, and the tone polite, nonpolemical, and precise. Interpreters were present but we often used only English. Generally speaking, all this was quite an extraordinary procedure for a Soviet representative, for he lives a much more withdrawn life than is usual for other diplomats and, again generally speaking, is not given to relaxed discussion with Western colleagues. The opportunity, therefore, to meet informally and at length with the Soviet representatives had a greater significance, at least potentially, than would have been the case with other diplomats.

The three Soviet co-chairmen with whom I held such meetings were all well-trained, capable, hard-working professionals, devoted Communists, able to take for granted their principles and the general lines of Soviet policy without having to use up all the time talking about them. Of the three, the highly placed Ambassador Zorin was the only one who was willing to agree to changes—including drafting changes of some substance—without having to refer to Moscow ahead of time, and the only one who seemed willing to initiate changes himself. In this he showed himself a very careful draftsman and analyst. Strict and formal in manner and seemingly not particularly affable by nature, he was always businesslike, courteous, and thoroughly informed, although he gave the impression, at least, that he regarded a matter of substance and the placing of a comma as equal in importance. Semyon K. Tsarapkin, who was not a member or candidate member of the Communist Party Central Committee, as were the others, was very courteous and pleasant, highly intelligent, but ultracautious. V. V. Kuznetsov, the Soviet First Deputy Foreign Minister, who had once studied at the Carnegie Institute of Technology and worked for the Ford Motor Company in Detroit, and was William C. Foster's opposite number at the Conference on Surprise Attack at Geneva in 1958, was outwardly the most affable and agreeable of the three, the one whose courteous personality and fluent English were most likely to appeal to Westerners on casual acquaintance. Actually he was a very tough-minded man in a working situation and, though always quite agreeable, was apparently not interested in initiating substantive changes or making any substantive effort to accommodate the Soviet point of view to that of others.

The co-chairmen's meetings were important, moreover, because it was possible there to exchange views on a continuing basis and in an informal way on a number of general problems beyond the immediate field of disarmament that were vexing to both the United States and the Soviet Union. Thus we spent many hours talking about our respective policies toward Germany and disarmament in relation to unification. Great effort went into explaining in detail the thinking behind our policy, how we were trying to avoid the mistakes which had been made in our treatment of the Weimar Republic, and why we thought that a healthy West Germany firmly attached to Western Europe and the United States was in the interest of both the United States and the Soviet Union. The Soviet representatives indicated at length their distrust and fear of the Germans in general and of our various proposals for a multilateral nuclear force (MLF) in NATO in particular, and their opposition to what they considered our policy of "arming" the German "warmongers" or "revanchists." They said nothing new but left no doubt of the depth of their conviction or of their distrust of the German role in NATO. Though in all our proposals we retained title to the nuclear warheads and control over their use, the Soviets bitterly opposed giving the West Germans any share, however limited, in NATO's nuclear policies and operations.

We also discussed various proposals for disengagement then current, such as the Rapacki Plan for making the two parts of Germany, Poland, and Czechoslovakia a nuclear-free zone. Since we could not have nuclear weapons in France, the proposal would have effectively eliminated U.S. tactical nuclear strength from Europe while not affecting those nuclear weapons or missiles inside the U.S.S.R. still fairly close to NATO countries. It is, of course, possible that the U.S.S.R. has ballistic missiles with nuclear warheads in East Germany, Poland, and Czechoslovakia, which would have to be removed if the proposed Rapacki Plan were complied with, but that would not offset the over-all damage to NATO's military position. At one point when the Soviet Co-chairman was asked whether the Soviet Union would consider withdrawing its troops from East Germany under such an arrangement, he replied categorically that it would not.

Such exchanges were useful, if not productive of tangible diplomatic progress. There were real and practical advantages in the co-chairmen's meetings: for working out a conference agenda in advance, for presentation of our proposals, and for the actual detailed drafting of texts. Here both sides could consider a draft and subject it to detailed discussion without the introduction of extraneous material or having to wait for fifteen other people to speak. We could and did discuss a whole range of questions relating to general and complete disarmament, particularly the differences between the American and Soviet draft proposals. Here we tried to clarify our respective positions on inspection and verification and on the gradual elimination of nuclear weapons and vehicles for their delivery. And we did produce some agreed texts.

One interesting example of the sort of discussions which we carried on concerned the number of annual on-site inspections of otherwise unidentified seismic events necessary for the successful operation of a comprehensive nuclear test-ban treaty and how such inspections might best be distributed.

Discussions were started in Geneva at the meetings on the test-ban treaty in March 1961, continued at an intensified pace at the United Nations during the General Assembly in the fall of 1961, were resumed at Geneva between the U.S.S.R., Great Britain, and the United States when the Eighteen-Nation Disarmament

Committee met, commencing in March 1962, and were continued again at the UN session in the fall of 1962.

The matter had already been discussed at length at various times and carefully reported to Washington by the summer of 1962. However, as a result of the research by the Project Vela underground and the publication of Soviet seismic statistics, we had prepared new maps of the Soviet Union of an accuracy and detail previously unavailable to our scientists. These maps made it clear that our earlier estimates of the number of earthquakes likely to occur in the heartland of the Soviet Union within a year had been too high. They also showed that for a long period practically all the earthquakes in the U.S.S.R. took place in three areas outside the industrialized Soviet heartland, which was the area Soviet representatives seemed most afraid would be the object of Western espionage under the guise of inspecting otherwise unidentified seismic events. On the basis of exchanges with Mr. Kuznetsov in the United States in the early part of October 1962, prior to the Cuban crisis which lasted from October 16, 1962, through October 28, 1962, I thought that further discussions on the basis of these seismological maps might be helpful. I obtained permission from Washington to show them to him at the United Nations, and did so at a meeting at which Alex Akalovsky of our delegation, who speaks fluent Russian, was present and kept careful notes of what we said. These notes were sent to Washington and to the President.

The possibility was very informally and tentatively suggested to Mr. Kuznetsov that, given new information on the incidence of earthquakes in the U.S.S.R., a satisfactory detection system might be developed by a combination of clustered arrays of seismographic instruments in deep holes which would be almost immune from extraneous noises, and of manned stations in the area of highest earthquake incidence. If such a system could be worked out, it might be possible in some way to prorate the quota of annual inspections of otherwise unidentified events between the seismic and nonseismic areas in the U.S.S.R. we were then discussing, so that there would be relatively few on-site inspections of otherwise unidentified seismic events in the industrialized heartland of that country.

Returning to the point in the latter part of October 1962, at another conference at which Alex Akalovsky was also present, I suggested that if the Soviet government were willing to exchange additional scientific data about earthquakes and on the speed at which seismic waves traveled through the earth in various Soviet areas, then perhaps instead of our insisting on an unconditional right to inspect any unidentified seismic event anywhere in the U.S.S.R. we might be able to work out my suggestion of some system of prorating inspections between agreed seismic and non-seismic areas. Thus, possibly, any unidentified seismic event in the Soviet industrialized heartland where no earthquakes had previously occurred might be deemed to have been nuclear in the absence of a satisfactory explanation. If there were no unidentified event, then there would be no need for on-site inspection in this area. We had six lengthy talks in English on this subject in the United States in October 1962, the last of these being on October 30, two days after the Cuban crisis was over. Mr. Kuznetsov seemed cordial and interested.

In another talk in early November 1962 I was able to tell Ambassador Kuznetsov that the United States might be willing to accept from eight to ten on-site inspections a year in the Soviet Union and from eight to ten nationally manned control posts on Soviet territory. Mr. Kuznetsov stated explicitly that this was too many and was not satisfactory. This was immediately reported to Washington.

At the same time we were discussing in a promising manner the possibility of arranging for a visit to the United States of a group of Soviet seismologists. Then, on November 7, 1962, Mr. Kuznetsov read me a letter from Premier Khrushchev, quite similar in content, apart from the references in that letter to the author and the President's scientific adviser, Dr. Jerome Wiesner, to the Premier's subsequent letter to President Kennedy of December 19, 1962,[13] in which the Premier stated that he would agree to an annual quota of two or three on-site inspections of otherwise unidentified events on all Soviet territory, ostensibly

---

[13] Richard P. Stebbins, ed., *Documents on American Foreign Relations, 1962* (New York: Harper & Row, for the Council on Foreign Relations, 1963), pp. 193-196.

on the basis of a suggestion of mine and of Dr. Wiesner's. It was pointed out in English by Mr. Akalovsky and myself to Deputy Foreign Minister Kuznetsov, who understood English perfectly, that no such suggestion had ever been made, and that the small number of annual on-site inspections of unidentified events suggested by Premier Khrushchev for all Soviet territory would be totally inadequate to meet the double purpose of inspection: first, actually to identify otherwise unidentified events and, second, to reassure public opinion and governments about unexplained events which might otherwise lead to a denunciation of the treaty.

There had been some, but not enough, scientific advances in our ability to detect and identify otherwise unidentified seismic events by distant instrumentation, so that the number of annual on-site inspections could be reduced somewhat, but not to two or three.[14] I again pointed out to Deputy Foreign Minister Kuznetsov that the annual number of on-site inspections of otherwise unidentified events had to be from eight to ten and that the total of three inspections per annum for all Soviet territory was not practical. Accordingly, the Khrushchev proposal, I stated, was quite unacceptable.

Deputy Foreign Minister Kuznetsov was so informed in very specific terms. At the same time he was advised of President Kennedy's deep interest in reaching an agreement on the nuclear test-ban treaty, and of our intensification of the Vela underground research program and our high hopes for this program. These exchanges ended this phase of the negotiations.[15]

Exchanges were resumed when William C. Foster, Director of ACDA, took them up at private negotiations with Ambassador Tsarapkin in New York in January 1963 after the receipt of Premier Khrushchev's letter of December 19, 1962, and following certain unofficial off-the-record talks by spokesmen for both sides.[16]

[14] Since on-site inspections of unidentified seismic events is so crucial, see the Note on pages 139-144, below, for a brief explanation of seismic detection through distant instrumentation.

[15] Because of the illness of some partners in his law firm, the author resigned as chairman of the U.S. delegation on December 31, 1962.

[16] Theodore C. Sorensen, *Kennedy* (New York: Harper & Row, 1965), p. 728.

Thus, there were no magic results from the meetings of the co-chairmen. Each man brought with him his own concepts, the goals of his government, and a realization of the basic differences between the two. But the meetings were a place for work and for sober discussion.

Disarmament and arms control measures are peculiarly matters for great-power consensus, and thus cannot be worked out in any other way, certainly not in large public conferences or at the UN General Assembly and its Disarmament Committee, by moral declamation, or by unilateral declarations with no policing machinery. The meetings of the co-chairmen opened up a forum where progress could be made and occasionally was made. But it was modest progress only, within the context of the existing global situation, especially the events relating to Cuba in October 1962.

Soviet Diplomatic Tactics

Throughout our experience of negotiations with the Soviets, we have come to discern a pattern of negotiating tactics which carries lessons for our diplomacy, on disarmament as on other matters. A Soviet diplomat, like a skilled chess player, does not expect his opposite number to give up something for nothing, not even a pawn. However valuable for getting press headlines, unexplained unilateral concessions by the West in the interest of stimulating reciprocal concessions only arouse his suspicion and concern. He puts in this category, moreover, any attempt to split the difference between two positions as a basis for compromise; he will take the concession as a sign of the other side's weakness and keep his own position frozen. As Philip E. Mosely put it, in an article which should be the *vade mecum* of Western diplomats, compromise "is alien to the Bolshevist way of thinking and to the discipline which the Communist Party has striven to inculcate in its members." The very word, he noted, is not native to the Russian language and is habitually used only in combination with the adjective "putrid."[17]

The Soviet diplomat will take advantage of any indiscretion or

[17] Philip E. Mosely, cited, p. 295.

mistake and will stretch or cut statements to fit his political bed of Procrustes as he wishes. Thus, for example, when Prime Minister Harold Macmillan was in Moscow in February 1959 he purportedly made a seemingly casual remark to Premier Khrushchev to the effect that Western insistence on on-site inspections in connection with the proposed nuclear test-ban treaty was being made primarily to satisfy American public opinion and that actually perhaps a fixed inspection quota of any symbolic number for on-site inspections of otherwise unidentified seismic events would be acceptable. As was readily to be expected, the Soviet government immediately seized on the low number of three as *the* number and rigidly proceeded from there without regard to the available scientific data on which our position was based.

Another example of the twisting technique was the handling of the conversations of October and November 1962, already described, in which the Soviets seized upon a nonexistent American proposal of an annual quota of two or three on-site inspections of unidentified events in a nonseismic area as a basis for an over-all agreement, though they knew perfectly well it was not. One must be prepared to resist this technique, no matter how long it may take or how often it may occur.

This brings us to another important point: the question of time. It came as a jolt during the immediate postwar period to find that Soviet diplomats often had quite a different concept of time from that of their Western counterparts. They were prepared to sit through meeting after meeting without getting anywhere, persistently repeating lines which those at the table came to know by heart. And the history of some of the conferences held at that time is rich in examples of misleading agreements which only multiplied the difficulties. It may be tempting to a Western government or diplomat, irritated by boredom or delay, to reach an agreement that merely papers over deep differences. But an agreement which does not rest on consensus and clear definitions may be worse than no agreement at all. Overeagerness only plays into Communist hands. It pays to listen, to be precise, determined, and willing to spend a lot of time, without any sign of being impatient, angry, or annoyed. One cannot negotiate successfully with Soviet representatives against a fixed deadline. Kurt Schumacher, the German Socialist leader, has been quoted as saying: "The day you Americans are as patient as the Russians, you will stop losing the cold war. And the day you learn to outsit them by a single minute, you will start winning it."[18]

This Soviet lack of concern for the passage of time seems to have two main explanations. For one thing, if the Soviet aim is not to agree but to obstruct agreement, as it was during much of the disarmament talks, then, of course, the passage of time only advances the goal. Furthermore, if delay is annoying to the adversary, there is the hope that the threat of further delay will so exhaust or provoke him or arouse public opinion in his country against a "do nothing" conference that he will be willing to make concessions that he would otherwise not have made in order to have a "successful" conference. In our co-chairmen's meetings at Geneva, for example, Deputy Foreign Minister Kuznetsov would occasionally discuss very pleasantly some point of Communist theory at great length, regardless of its relevance to the matter at hand. The other explanation may lie in the Marxist-Leninist concept, now worn somewhat thin, that time and history are on the Communists' side: thus the terms of any agreement sought tend to become ever more favorable to the Soviet side as the making of the agreement is delayed. Practically, things might not always work out that way, because the "march to the victory of socialism over capitalism" has its periods of retrenchment and tactical retreat as well as of advance. But the almost religious Marxian conviction, of which they now may not be so sure, that the general trend is in their favor undoubtedly affects the character of Soviet diplomacy.

Then there is the pitfall of the "agreement in principle," which was already a serious danger in wartime negotiations with the Soviets. Time and again—and certainly this is clear in the Soviet insistence on an agreement on disarmament first, with details of inspection and such matters to come later—Soviet negotiators will press for a general agreement, often on a principle, such as being for "peace," to which it is very difficult to

[18] Charles W. Thayer, *Diplomat* (New York: Harper & Row, 1959), p. 96.

object, and will charge bad faith when this is refused. They are aware of the impatience of their Western counterparts and seek to make agreement seem very close by stressing how easy it would be to record it in general terms. By pushing in this way, they hope for an agreement of such vagueness that they will be able to interpret it in their own way and act to their own advantage while professing to observe the agreement. We have only to remember the disputes about the Yalta and Potsdam agreements to realize what this can mean.

We in the West have been trained to pay attention to facts and concrete details, to reason from the particular to the general, and to build agreement on this basis; otherwise, we believe, any agreement will break down in practice. The Soviet diplomat is less concerned with agreements as legal instruments; he does not stress the factual basis but seeks an advantageous political position. This is not to imply that Soviet interest does not at some times require a detailed, hardheaded agreement. It is just to point out that at other times it may be otherwise. We must not allow ourselves to be taken in, especially in matters of disarmament and arms control, where we need extremely specific and detailed agreements and verification controls if we are not to imperil our security. Any idea of agreeing to general propositions as an encouragement to compromises on crucial matters of detail would be folly.

There is also a basic difference in how the term "in principle" is construed. To an Englishman and an American an agreement "in principle" is one based on the practical steps which the diplomat believes he can carry out in time—perhaps not in every detail but in broad outline. On the continent, including the U.S.S.R., however, an agreement "in principle" does not mean an agreement which can and will be eventually carried out. Rather it represents a common point of view at which the two still divergent viewpoints might ultimately converge if it suits either side to do so in the light of conditions existing at the time performance is required. There is no commitment to proceed. It is essential that we understand this fundamental distinction clearly, for there has been much bitterness and misunderstanding when we have not.

The "agreement in principle" approach, if successful, is often followed by the "waiving" argument. That is, the Soviet diplomat will claim that, by not pursuing a matter of detail or a specific point at the time when the general agreement "in principle" was made, the diplomat "waived" it for all time. It was to avoid this gambit that Mr. McCloy and I, with the approval of President Kennedy and Secretary of State Rusk, took the action we did in connection with the Joint Statement of Agreed Principles, as explained above.

Patience, persistence, calm toughness of mind, a nature impervious to insults, a constantly creative and resourceful mind, and unwillingness to be discouraged are all essential characteristics for the Western negotiator. He should have calculated, well-thought-out, and creatively formulated positions; an alertness to negotiate the possible without sacrificing essentials; and then a determination to sit it out as long as necessary. But if science advances or other concrete conditions change, then we should be prepared to adapt our positions accordingly. It does not pay to present proposals designed solely or mainly for the purpose of putting the other side "on the spot," for such a design is readily discernible and therefore usually boomerangs.

Other nations can figure out as quickly as the originators of such proposals just what their character is and whether anything real or substantial is actually being proposed. Indeed, it could be said that our proposal to the Soviet Union to transfer fissionable material in equal or nearly equal amounts for peaceful purposes fits the description of a propaganda move. For we have never made public, so far as I know, what our total store of this material is and how it compares with the Soviet stockpile. Many people in other countries believe, perhaps cynically, that if this proposal really hurt us we would not have made it.

There are those who strongly disagree with this point of view. But it seems to me we are on firmer ground if we make clear to all that we advance only those honest proposals which we can ourselves live with and carry out wholeheartedly if they are adopted.[19] Throughout my service as a negotiator I have endeavored to advocate or advance only proposals which, in my

[19] For a somewhat different viewpoint, see Fred Charles Iklé, *How Nations Negotiate* (New York: Harper & Row, 1964), especially pp. 248-253, but compare pp. 87 ff.

estimation, met these conditions. I do not relish being hoist by our own petard, which so often happens when you are trying to show up the other fellow before the "bar of world opinion." The devious Oriental diplomat, so elegantly described by Harold Nicolson in his book on diplomacy, has no place on an American delegation. As Sir Harold remarked, "It is advisable . . . for the Westerner to stick always to truth, in the expenditure of which he possesses ample reserves."[20] Or as the old adage puts it, "If you tell the truth, you don't have to remember anything."[21]

Even in talks between hostile nations outright lies do not pay off. As President Kennedy said on October 22, 1962, in announcing the blockade against the Soviet missiles in Cuba: "Neither the United States of America nor the world community of nations can tolerate deliberate deception and offensive threats. . . ." Contrary to general opinion, it does not pay for a diplomat to bluff. Khrushchev found that out in 1958-61 when he failed over four years to carry out his threats that he would sign a separate peace treaty with East Germany in a stated period of time unless the Allies agreed to some major concessions on West Berlin.

[20] *Diplomacy* (London: Oxford University Press, 1963), p. 255.
[21] Samuel Clemens, *Mark Twain's Notebook* (New York: Harper, 1935), p. 240.

Chapter III

Verification and Inspection

Disarmament is no game of blindman's buff. Reasonably reliable verification is the *sine qua non* for any disarmament proposals which are seriously meant. It is so important, and has so often been the sticking point in negotiations both on the test ban and on general disarmament, that it merits full discussion by itself before those two subjects are taken up. Lack of provision for verification is often a clear signal that a proposal has a goal other than disarmament in view: propaganda, perhaps, or the protection of a national interest considered more urgent than disarmament itself. In Soviet eyes protection of the national system of secrecy appears to be such an interest, overriding anything to be gained by agreed measures to control armaments.

It is necessary to be clear about verification, both in general and in regard to the difficulties the Western nations have had with the Soviet Union on the subject. As is only too well known, the two sides have for years been at loggerheads over an issue of verification, that of on-site inspection on Soviet territory. The heavy emphasis which has been given to this conflict, which occurs in relation both to general disarmament and to a comprehensive test ban, has resulted in a distorted focus on verification in all its facets. Too many people think of verification solely as a matter of identifying violations through on-site inspection by human inspectors. Actually, the term is much broader than that, the methods much more varied, and the disagreement not completely total.

As the term is used now, verification may perform three major functions. It may protect parties to a general or limited disarmament accord or test ban by apprising them of violations. Second, it may provide reassurance that an agreement has been or is being carried out. And it may deter violations by making them too difficult, too expensive, or politically too risky. If things go well, it is to be hoped that the reassurance and deterrence aspects of verification will move into the foreground, while the violation aspects will become less important.

Defined in this general way, it is clear that verification and attempts at deceit are as old as man's history. There has never been a government which has not sought to keep its eye on states whose actions were important to it or to conceal its own defenses or armaments. Many national devices have been developed to get such information about others, ranging from the careful reading of "open" material and regular diplomatic reporting to the use of espionage. Such verification is going on all the time, assisted by increasingly efficient scientific marvels of the contemporary age. Indeed, the world is in a time of expanding technological possibilities as far as instruments for verification are concerned, as our ability to launch far earth, solar, and space satellites illustrates. The policy maker must constantly review his proposals in the light of new scientific developments in this field. Our proposal in 1962 for a partial test-ban treaty without international inspection was, as has been explained above, partly the result of new scientific developments in instruments of detection and identification and in the verification of explosions occurring in different environments and from different causes, whether natural or man-made. In a number of cases, so-called "nonintrusive" verification by the adversary party from his national territory is all that is called for, and here there is no deep conflict between the Soviet Union and the United States.

International Inspection, the Stumbling Block

The conflict arises on the issue of inspection by foreigners, whether representing another state or an international body, within the territory of one of the parties to a proposed agreement —though not in all instances of such inspection. Verification by foreign observers of specific acts at specific locations in the Soviet Union seemed to fall within the limits of the acceptable for the Soviet negotiators, at least in the abstract. The Soviet Draft Treaty on General and Complete Disarmament of March 1962 provided that inspectors of the proposed International Disarmament Organization should observe the destruction of certain specific weapons, the dismantling of certain stated productive facilities, the liquidation of specified bases, the discontinuance of certain types of production, the withdrawal of foreign troops from abroad, the demobilization of agreed numbers of military personnel, and the destruction of prelaunch rocket facilities at selected sites.[1] These definite acts at specific places were the only things to be observed. There was no provision for any further inspection should suspicion of violations be aroused, nor any provision for inspection to make sure that the level of armaments retained was what had been designated as the legal maximum.

Even in this limited area, however, Soviet representatives do not seem to want to go into the kind of detail that can lead to confidence and firm agreement. We inquired repeatedly at Geneva, but without obtaining satisfactory answers, whether provision would be made against the prior "cannibalization" of weapons to be destroyed. In a "bomber bonfire," for example, would the role of the inspectors be confined merely to counting the actual number of aircraft destroyed or would there be opportunity for independent assurance that the bombers to be burned still had their full complement of instruments and that they were not merely empty shells, stripped of all essentials? In other words, would there be a real obligation to destroy modern weapons in good condition or could unusable ones with missing parts be included in the total number required to be destroyed? There are other fundamentally important questions of this seemingly minor nature, termed "quibbling details" and "espionage" by Soviet representatives and "bickering" or annoying "legalisms" by part of our press, including some of the same critics who had been quick to object to the alleged lack of specificity in the

[1] Richard P. Stebbins, ed., *Documents on American Foreign Relations, 1962* (New York: Harper & Row, for the Council on Foreign Relations, 1963), pp. 89-115.

Korean armistice of July 27, 1953. But the careful negotiator interested in a fair and adequate system of disarmament must think out and discuss these matters in precise and workable terms in advance of agreement, or after the event be labeled a fool, incompetent, or worse if the Soviets or the Chinese Communists make mockery of the agreement.

It is not that the West is seeking some mathematically absolute standard of reliable verification. We know we are dealing with politics and not mathematics. The definition of "reliability" becomes, therefore, a matter of judging the political context and of balancing the political alternatives, goals, and risks, all in line with the methods of verification which science has made available at a given point in time. It is not realistic to ask whether a verification system will be 100 per cent foolproof, which it probably will not be, but whether our relative strength and position are such that we could afford to run the risk of some small violations in order to achieve political or other goals we consider valuable to us and to the free world. In the partial nuclear test-ban treaty of 1963, in view of the very real scientific advances in the launching of far earth and solar satellites and in undersea detection capabilities, we did feel we could afford to run the risks that were involved.

The situation in regard to stage-by-stage disarmament, however, would be significantly different. In an advanced stage of disarmament, both of weapons and of production facilities, the political and military risks of even small-scale violations could be so acute that stringent measures of verification, including on-site inspection for retained levels of armaments, would be required. They would be needed in addition to really adequate peace-keeping institutions free from a veto by an interested party in the Security Council or from a majority vote in the General Assembly against the taking of necessary action, especially by countries located in the area concerned.

The United States has shown considerable flexibility and a willingness to adjust its proposals and negotiating positions as scientific change has opened new doors. As has already been pointed out, we introduced a partial test-ban treaty in three environments in August 1962 which relied upon national detection instruments and national policing. And on the matter of on-site inspection for the identification of "suspicious" underground explosions, we have also modified our position as new methods in seismology and new facilities for detection and identification resulting from intensified study made it possible for us to do so without risk of endangering national security. Thus, in the course of negotiations on a compehensive test-ban treaty, we agreed to certain limitations on the freedom of movement of inspectors on their way to on-site inspections; we moved from a position supporting a network of internationally operated and manned control stations to acceptance of internationally supervised and nationally manned stations. We also drastically reduced the number of stations proposed as we improved the character of the equipment available for monitoring work; we moved also from an insistence on international inspection to a system of reciprocal inspection by the two sides; and in 1963 we turned to a more favorable consideration of automated control stations supplemented by a certain degree of direct inspection by official observers. Most important of all, we removed the threshold of 4.75 in the seismic, logarithmic scale of magnitude on prohibited seismic nuclear events and agreed in our proposed treaty to prohibit *all* nuclear underground tests, however small, a step which vastly complicates the problem of detection and identification because of the ever-present background noise.

In the only instance in which there has been any detailed discussion of the matter, the Soviet attitude toward on-site inspection by foreign inspectors has been impossibly restrictive. Although Premier Khrushchev at various times seemed to approve of the idea of on-site inspection, it was always in such limited terms of practicality that Western rejection could be predicted. In effect, the Soviet view throughout a long and tangled history of talks and negotiations can be summed up in one short sentence: The only good inspector is a Soviet inspector. All our efforts, including much scientific research, to meet Soviet objections to on-site inspections of otherwise unidentified seismic events in the test-ban talks have so far met with no success. Nor did similar efforts in the negotiations on disarmament lead to any better results; there we emphasized that inspectors would be stationed at major production facilities and not given freedom to roam, and we introduced the idea of a zonal inspection system with the inspecting side free to choose the zone to be inspected but otherwise restricted to inspection only within that zone.

The unshakable fact of the matter is that the Soviet Union has thus far been determined not to allow foreign inspectors on its territory, except perhaps to witness the destruction of agreed material. One might go into a highly detailed history of the disarmament and test-ban talks and into an analysis of Soviet character, but the result would come out the same. Indeed, so strongly held is this Soviet position that it throws into question even the "one-shot" inspections now provided for in the Soviet draft treaty on general disarmament. One cannot tell, but certainly the Soviet attitude toward on-site inspections in the nuclear test-ban and disarmament negotiations does not lead to a very lively optimism as to what can be effectively accomplished in the field of disarmament verification.

The Roots of Soviet Opposition

If reliable verification is, from our point of view, the cornerstone on which any structure of disarmament or arms control must rest, then we must consider in a realistic way the question of what, if any, type of verification beyond the purely national methods available might be acceptable to the Soviet Union and still meet the requirements of the United States. Perhaps the simplest initial approach is to see what Soviet representatives have themselves stated their government would *not* accept.

As we have seen, they have made it absolutely clear that, with the few exceptions noted above, on-site inspections by foreign observers are ruled out; also, that there can be no inspection of retained levels of armaments. One might reasonably suppose that if we understood the reasons for these policies and the attitudes behind them, we might have some chance of changing them. A great deal has been written to explain this Soviet distaste and, indeed, fear of foreign inspection or intrusion. It is attributed to historical distrust of the foreigner, to a suspicious "peasant mentality," to the memories of foreign invasions, and even to the nineteenth-century controversy between those Russians who wanted to Europeanize the country and those who insisted on the special mission of Slavic Russia. Soviet officials argued that there would, under our proposals, be no binding agreement on our part to carry out and complete the disarmament process once we had discovered through inspection their launching sites, since our proposals do not envision automatic transition from one stage to the next.

Perhaps these elements may have some influence on current Soviet thinking, but working with and observing Soviet representatives over an extensive period of negotiation has convinced me that this reluctance—or fixation—has somewhat different roots. What is involved here is a kind of "parallel track" situation, one track involving policy and the other attitudes.

On the one track are certain rational policy considerations, such as the benefit to be derived from keeping strict military secrecy. Added to the emphasis on secrecy as a "good" in itself is the often expressed fear that the West wants in Stage I of disarmament to ascertain Soviet missile-launching sites and, having acquired this knowledge, will then engage in pre-emptive attack on the U.S.S.R. instead of going on to Stages II and III.

It may be argued that excess secrecy is a double-edged policy and that it can boomerang by stimulating the adversary to greater efforts to overcome a supposed deficiency which actually does not exist. This was the case with the so-called "missile gap," of which so much was heard in the late 1950s and during the election campaign of 1960. However the calculation may turn out, it seems clear that the Soviet Union, for the time being at least, considers its secrecy a military asset. If this were all that is involved, then one might look ahead to a possible change in policy as photographic and other satellites penetrate the area which a nation may hope to keep secret.

There is, however, much more to the Soviet fear of intrusion than a desire to safeguard military secrecy. The second of the parallel tracks is one of attitudes. There is, first of all, an apparently bottomless suspicion which springs from the dogmatic Communist assumption of hostility from the outside world. This attitude is combined with a belief in the inherent superiority of the "socialist" system, seasoned by a considerable lack of knowledge of the reality of what they call the capitalist or imperialist world. The dogma of unending struggle, together with an internal system which requires keeping total control of the Soviet population, leads to the extreme and protective emphasis on national sovereignty which permeates Soviet concepts of international law and many aspects of Soviet foreign policy.

At the same time, the Soviet official is aware of the gap between the premises of his system and its actual accomplishment. This gap he desires to hide from what he considers to be hostile and prying eyes. It is an attitude that suffuses the whole Soviet system and extends to all aspects of life which might expose to a foreigner weaknesses, popular discontent, or contradictions between reality and official propaganda. A foreign inspector, though representing an international agency, would be bound to see more than just the weapon or the factory that he is inspecting. So he becomes as "dangerous" as any other outsider.

It has often been pointed out, and with justice, that the Soviet system, with emphasis on a single loyalty and a single truth, must be suspicious of alien, so-called cosmopolitan or objective influences. Generally speaking, it seeks to protect its citizens from contact with them. Recent so-called liberalizing tendencies within the Soviet Union have not really produced any significant changes in this regard, though they justify awaiting the future with some curiosity. When tourists and diplomats are allowed to travel only along certain well-defined routes, and when a Professor Barghoorn can, in Soviet eyes legitimately, be accused of espionage,[2] it is not realistic to expect the Soviet Union to accept foreign inspectors who would come with official sanction as representatives of a foreign body, and with a function of independently judging acts of the Soviet government, which no Soviet citizen has the right to do.

Finally, in addition to the assumption of hostility and the matter of preserving a single loyalty, there is the emphasis on compartmentalized knowledge. Restrictions on information per-

[2] Professor Frederick Barghoorn of Yale, a noted authority on the Soviet Union, was arrested on charges of espionage in the U.S.S.R. on October 31, 1963, and released on November 16, 1963.

vade the entire system. The citizen is not kept informed, as we would define the term; some information is doled out to him, or he may find out things for himself; but generally information is made available only on a narrowly interpreted "need to know" basis, with even high officials aware of only a part of the total picture. Again, in such a system an independent inspector from abroad cannot find a natural place and would meet hostility, not cooperation.

What Openings for Agreement?

This listing of factors which lie behind Soviet hostility and exclusiveness is relevant when one asks the question: What can the United States do, if anything, to change such an exclusive attitude and to promote the development of one more receptive to proposals that could conceivably lead to mutually acceptable and workable agreements? Unfortunately, there is no dramatic, simple answer either for policy or for attitudes.

Dealing with attitudes is at best a tricky business, with no guarantee that a particular measure may not have an unexpected and undesired effect. The most promising approach, obviously a long-range one, might be a search for ways to make Soviet leaders more at ease with representatives of other cultures and societies and more aware of what those societies are in actuality rather than in Soviet mythology. Exchanges of key persons might be of value, as well as joint efforts to study certain problems of relevance to both American and Soviet society. Expanded trade relations as recommended by President Johnson's committee on East-West trade may have certain favorable results beyond the purely economic ones.[3] Expanded scientific cooperation and exchanges of information might also be helpful. But a caveat must be entered. Past experience has shown that there is no way of telling whether such exchanges will result in greater sensitivity or greater hostility. They hold no certain promise of really reducing the dimensions of the problem. In the final analysis there is little

[3] *Report to the President of the Special Committee on U.S. Trade Relations with Eastern European Countries and the Soviet Union* (Washington: The White House, April 29, 1965).

that the United States can do directly to influence attitudes in the Soviet Union on such matters as loyalty to outworn dogma, world outlook, and the resort to secrecy, so long as Moscow's basic approach is what it is. As Soviet leaders do not cease to tell us, and as we have found out from experience, "peaceful coexistence" does not apply on the ideological front or to wars of "national liberation."

As for influencing Soviet policy on disarmament and arms control to move in a direction closer to our own so that some accord may be possible, here again we are confronted with a number of unanswerable questions. We cannot be certain, for example, that efforts at increased friendliness will lead to increased harmony on policy. Indeed, it may well be argued that the Cuban crisis contributed heavily toward creating the atmosphere in the Soviet Union which led to the signing of the partial nuclear test-ban treaty in 1963, though it should also not be forgotten that by proposing purely national instruments of verification, as we did in August 1962 at Geneva, we removed a major obstacle to such an agreement from the Soviet point of view. On balance, it seems to me that, although we did take a number of steps at Geneva which made it possible to seize the opportunity to work out the test-ban agreement, these were only peripherally relevant to the hardheaded calculations that must have gone on in the Kremlin. The Soviet calculations must have dealt at least with the rift with China, reunification and possible nuclear arming of Germany, leadership of the world Communist movement, developments in the "third world," domestic pressures for a reallocation of resources, military-industrial demands, and the general strategy the Soviet government wanted to adopt toward the United States.

From all these considerations it follows that our best chance of influencing the direction of Soviet policy lies in being true to ourselves, forming our policy according to our own needs and those of the free world, explaining our goals patiently to Soviet representatives, and honestly refraining from actions which contradict the explanations. We must also take care to maintain the position of power without which the Soviet leaders would have no interest in talking about disarmament with us at all.

Within this framework we are free to pick those measures

which we think have the best chance of success in advancing us toward our goals. Fortunately, in the last few years we have been able to focus much of our discussion with the Soviet Union on more limited measures of disarmament and arms control and, therefore, to press more strenuously for measures which would seem to have a far better chance for adoption than would the infinitely complicated and ambitious proposals for a comprehensive treaty on general and complete disarmament.

Considering the prospects solely from the standpoint of the verification needed and of the likelihood that such verification would be mutually acceptable to the United States and the Soviet Union, it seems clear that, at least temporarily, measures requiring numerous and elaborate on-site inspections with ambitious schemes for international teams of inspectors, as well as proposals for the inspection of retained levels of armaments, should be placed in the icebox. Nor do arrangements depending on the detailed examination of budgets or production records seem to hold much promise as yet. Although we should always remain alert for changes in attitude and policy on the part of the Soviet Union, for the present there appears little chance that it would agree to any of the above proposals or that any such agreement would be realistic in practice.

Since we are interested in moving further along the road to agreement on measures of arms control and disarmament, let us then pick out and concentrate on those which are both acceptable to us and which we think might, with patient negotiation, come to be acceptable to the Soviet Union. Among such measures are the following:

1. *The destruction of specified obsolete (or other) weaponry.* Such measures would involve short-term inspection at specified sites, such as the Soviet Union itself has proposed.

2. *The inspection of atomic reactors on a mutual basis.* In 1964 President Johnson announced that he would open an atomic reactor at Rowe, Massachusetts, to inspection by the International Atomic Energy Agency (IAEA), in hopes that this gesture would stimulate a reciprocal Soviet step. This inspection has been made. That the Soviet Union has not reciprocated is not surprising, in the light of our earlier discussion. We should, how-

ever, consider trying for reciprocal visits by inspection teams from the United States and the Soviet Union, on the theory that such inspection may not be considered intrusive and that it should not be difficult to set in motion. At any rate, it is something worth trying.

3. *Transfer of fissionable material to peaceful use under control of the IAEA by both the United States and the Soviet Union.* This step would not require any inspection, but just the recording of the transfer of the material and the setting up of safeguards for its use.

4. *The exploration of a verified freeze of the number and characteristics of strategic nuclear offensive and defensive vehicles.* Detailed information could be submitted by both sides, but some inspection would still be necessary.

5. *Prevention of the further proliferation of nuclear weapons.* A number of steps might be taken here which would not involve inspection within either the Soviet Union or the United States, though controls over international transportation and possibly inspection in other areas would be required. In this connection it might be useful to examine further the possibility of establishing regional "atom-free" zones complete with operating on-site inspection schemes which do not give either side an advantage. For reasons already mentioned in the preceding chapter, the Rapacki Plan for such a zone in Central Europe is not acceptable. Carefully chosen denuclearized zones elsewhere, however, might serve as useful laboratories in the field in which we have much to learn. Above all, we should never lose sight of the goal, a treaty to prevent the spread of nuclear weapons.

6. *A comprehensive test-ban treaty.* With advances in our Vela program, it is possible that we are approaching a time when we will be able to place greater reliance on more sophisticated "national" instruments of detection even for the identification of "suspicious" underground events, which are not covered by the existing treaty. If things develop in this way, we might be able to cut even further the requirement for on-site inspection that we now find necessary.

7. *Establishment of observation posts to prevent or reduce the likelihood of surprise attack.* Such posts might be established

outside the territories of the two major powers, in which case there might be inspection of disquieting developments or rumors of military moves and deployments by teams composed of U.S. and Soviet personnel, plus some members from the territories actually being inspected. To be meaningful, the system must provide for sufficient mobility for the inspectors so that they could actually carry out their duties; they should also have free channels of communication with the authorities to which they are responsible, without hindrance from or the necessary approval of the territorial sovereign.

These measures, which are discussed more fully in later chapters, are listed here merely to indicate where, in view of the negative Soviet policy on inspection, the more promising steps may perhaps be taken.

On the other hand, measures calling for a freeze on production or a large-scale reduction in atomic material production or a major reduction of weaponry, though desirable for a number of reasons, seem certain to run into stern Soviet objections because of the degree and type of verification that the Western states would require. We now know that there was opposition within the Soviet government even to Khrushchev's concluding the very modest partial nuclear test-ban treaty of 1963, where no international inspection was provided. How much more opposition there would be to a more ambitious scheme, we cannot say. But it is difficult to see any likely modification of the Soviet position, whether the inspection proposed is international or reciprocal. It would still involve an obvious, visible, and apparently unacceptable foreign intrusion.

The above suggestions are based on the assumption, which I firmly hold, that it is desirable to continue to seek further agreement on arms control and disarmament, provided we do not allow ourselves to be foolishly lulled in the process. We must not allow history to continue to point to 1963 as the year of our greatest achievement. Furthermore, should there be a further agreement involving the beginnings of inspection, it might be most helpful in showing how inspection worked out in practice, how "intrusive" it would actually be, how much of a burden, and how much "espionage" was really involved. Let us remember that, in spite of all the discussion and thought that have gone into the working out of inspection schemes, no one has actually lived with one. No one really knows how it would work out. *Both* sides, the United States as well as the U.S.S.R., would have to learn to live with foreign inspections on their territory. Would we actually accept Soviet inspection on our soil in practice?

Such experience would be useful in any event. Possibly it might help the Soviets to begin to overcome some of the fears which they now have of verification as a threat to their security.

In our preparatory work on the nuclear test-ban treaty, moreover, comparatively little attention was paid to the tremendous costs and logistical difficulties that would be involved in organizing and mounting even one on-site inspection underground for a suspicious event in the remote reaches of possibly frozen soil in Siberia: a large team of specialists plus servicing personnel, a great number of specialized instruments, heavy digging equipment, possibly nuclear-powered electrical generators, plus living equipment and food, all of which would most probably have to be airlifted, protected, and preserved. This is not to say that with cooperation such difficulties could not be surmounted. But it has seemed to me that some of the advocacy of large numbers of annual on-site inspections of otherwise unidentified events has been a bit on the casual side and has ignored the actual logistics involved in the terrain, the climate, the mining techniques, and the necessary pipeline of stores.

Every small change in some way alters the entire context within which agreement will have to be sought. Because the question of verification is so important, we must seek out expertly, patiently, and unemotionally every possible break in the impasse as we proceed step by step in trying to deal with the enormous problems of disarmament and arms control. That is why it is so important to support the excellent work of the Arms Control and Disarmament Agency.

Chapter IV

Disarmament and Arms Control

It is fair to say that since 1946 the U.S. government has expended more man-hours and more effort on questions of disarmament and arms control than on any other one subject of international negotiation in a comparable period of time. We have explored a host of alternatives, from immediate and limited proposals to reduce the risks of the current arms race to theoretical studies of keeping the peace in a disarmed world. We have considered formal agreements and also the possibilities of action by "mutual example." We have discussed these matters in the United Nations, at Geneva, and elsewhere, with our allies and our adversaries. Through it all we have echoed the age-old refrain, probably heard every time a new and horrendous weapon is introduced, that this time the chicken-egg conundrum of armaments and security must be solved. The only difference is that if we fail now, we may not have another chance to set our feet firmly on the right path.

How much progress have we made? To take the briefest tally of a complicated subject, there has been no approach to agreement with the Soviet Union on the core issues of general and complete disarmament, or even on limited measures for arms control, such as safeguards against surprise attack. On the other hand, we were able in 1963 to reach agreement on three limited matters which, though not technically disarmament measures, could help to set the scene for further agreements which might ultimately lead to disarmament: the so-called "hot line," the partial test ban, and the resolution against placing nuclear weapons in outer space, all to be discussed later. And 1964 was the year of the mutual example, involving such steps as cutting back the production of fissionable material. Of limited inherent and indeed even practical value, nevertheless they held some promise for the future. Both logic and practice make it clear that the more immediate possibilities lie with limited measures. No matter how necessary or how sincerely desired and worked for, general and complete disarmament is a far-off will-o'-the-wisp.

This candid statement of a frustrating truth might need no elaboration were it not for the difficulty many well-intentioned people seem to have in accepting it. For understandable and irreproachable reasons people and nations yearn to avoid war, especially war among the big powers. Being human, they all too often eagerly embrace a slogan or a single concept as a kind of magical prescription to ensure the condition which they seek and are bitterly disillusioned when, for want of having been thought through, the prescription doesn't work. For many, disarmament is such a prescription; like "the end of colonialism" for the emerging nations, it is supposed to achieve an earthly paradise, and quickly, if governments only would see the light and accept it. To add to the confusion, the careful, responsible, and well-thought-out approach of the Western governments is equated in some minds with unwillingness to work for peace, or even indeed with "imperialism" or "colonialism," just because it addresses itself to all the real questions of international life and power and offers no easy panacea.

As a result, disarmament has become a magnet for emotional exaggeration and for overblown and deceiving propaganda, and for an equally foolish belief that all the sums now spent on the design and production of armaments in a particular country could somehow magically be turned over to help the underdeveloped nations. Actually, these sums represent results in scientific advance, research, space exploration, buildings, laboratories, employment, taxes, and earnings. And, to avoid economic chaos, these sums would have to remain largely within the particular country involved even if arms production were stopped altogether.

Conditions for Disarmament

How much simpler it would be if there were more general awareness and understanding of four basic realities about disarmament. (1) The essential foundation for negotiation on arms control and disarmament is respectable military strength on both sides. (2) Disarmament is as much a function of national security as is armament. (3) Limited measures may open the way to general disarmament, while being of value in themselves. (4) There is no reason to assume that disarmament in and of itself will bring with it the disappearance of conflict any more than has the defeat of the Axis powers or the "end of colonialism."

Let us start with the matter of the "respectable military strength" on both sides. Like the arms race itself, the impulsion to negotiate for the control or abolition of arms by consent is rooted in a mutual respect among adversaries for each other's military strength. This is not to say that so-called "peripheral" or militarily weak nations may not be involved in disarmament talks. They are usefully involved at Geneva and at the United Nations. But there would be no talks at all were it not for the fact that both the United States (with Canada and its European allies) and the Soviet Union (and its allies) consider it a worthwhile goal of foreign policy to seek to reduce the military threat posed by the other. It is this respect which forms the compelling reason for the consideration of disarmament.

Two conclusions follow. First, unilateral measures of disarmament or multilateral measures which inequitably bear on only one side and which thus undermine the condition of mutual respect to the detriment of that side will most likely lead not to acceptable disarmament but to the political defeat of the weakened side and probably also to greater dangers to peace. The break-up of disarmament talks, for which there would no longer be a *raison d'être,* would follow. Thus the most ardent and the most emotional supporters of disarmament, the impatient ones who argue for unreciprocated unilateral or unbalanced measures on the grounds that they will help to create the necessary confidence and inspire the other side to reply in kind, are in reality the worst enemies of any realistic disarmament. Unreciprocated measures would ultimately destroy the basis on which the negotiation of stable agreements rests.

The second conclusion stems from the first. If the basis of disarmament talks has been correctly stated, then it follows that disarmament can only proceed on the principle of balance, whereby the stock of existing arms and those from future production are reciprocally reduced without altering in any drastic way the existing relationship between the states concerned. If, on the other hand, a disarmament proposal would, in its practical effect, result in a considerable weakening of one side as against the other, then such a proposal may be considered an element of political warfare and not a serious disarmament effort. The U.S. Draft Outline of a Treaty on General and Complete Disarmament in a Peaceful World, submitted on April 18, 1962, is, by and large, animated by the principle of balance.[1] The Soviet Draft Treaty on General and Complete Disarmament under Strict International Control, of March 15, 1962, is regrettably animated to a large extent by the quest for unilateral Soviet advantage.[2]

To say that disarmament is as much a function of national security as is armament is to recognize that both vitally affect the existence of nations and also their ability to carry out international responsibilities, including the keeping of the peace in a disarming and disarmed world. This simple proposition is much ignored. Even among the non-Communist members of the Eighteen-Nation Disarmament Committee, for example, there are those who have impatiently advocated speed in dismantling the defenses of the West and have brushed aside efforts to ensure specificity in the agreements as unnecessary and even deliberately provocative. It should be noted that these states often do not advocate equal speed in their own disarmament or in solving their own regional disputes. Nor do many of them refrain from asking for U.S. military aid or economic aid for projects which release their own funds for armaments. These remarks are not

[1] Richard P. Stebbins, ed., *Documents on American Foreign Relations, 1962* (New York: Harper & Row, for the Council on Foreign Relations, 1963), pp. 115-147.

[2] Same, pp. 89-115.

16420

made to be querulous or critical but merely to point out that the intimate connection between national security and disarmament clicks into focus easily enough when it is one's own problems that are involved, as in the case of India's and Pakistan's concern with Kashmir. It is only too easy to advocate rapid disarmament by someone else. And it may be that recent developments outside the main arms race, such as Communist China's attack on India in late 1962, Peking's advancing nuclear weapons program, and its support of the Viet Cong and North Viet-Nam, will make it harder for New Delhi to advocate quick disarmament when either Washington or Moscow or both may be called on for help in the event of trouble.

To put it another way, it is clear that no matter what the propagandists say, disarmament is not the first priority goal of any government in the world today. This priority everywhere goes to the protection of the national security. In the case of the United States, a major aspect of that security is the maintenance of an international environment in which we and our friends can live in peace and freedom. This is the simple reality of our times. There is no point in wasting time fulminating against it. The real, the significant question in disarmament is not which should come first, defense or disarmament, but how to utilize both defense and disarmament in their manifold interrelationships to attain security and peace. The U.S. draft outline of April 1962 was a clear, intelligent, hardheaded attempt to come to grips with this central question. If it has not fully done that, then let us re-examine it.

What has been said above should not be misconstrued as an argument against disarmament. Not at all. It is intended only to point out that disarmament cannot safely be the subject of vague, hopeful, unanchored agreements. Like defense policy, it has to be specific. Indeed, although I have the lawyer's acute awareness both of the paralyzing effect that excessive textual detail may have on the carrying out of agreements and of the maxim that the letter killeth where the spirit giveth life, I am nevertheless convinced that in disarmament matters a clearly elaborated agreement is the only kind of agreement into which any responsible leader sincerely interested in disarmament can enter. The architects of a disarmament treaty have to be careful, and being careful in this instance demands precise detail written into the terms of the agreement itself. The Soviet penchant for "agreements in principle" has been much in evidence in the disarmament talks, but such agreements—which avoid hard thinking—must be spurned. They can be nothing but a trap. We must know what all the parties to a disarmament agreement are expected to do and when, what their rights and reciprocal obligations are, and what happens if certain obligations are not carried out. If the exact details in a matter so vital as disarmament are not worked out ahead of time, suspicion, distrust, and endless wrangling and misunderstanding will result, with increasing tension, setbacks, and accusations of bad faith as their companions.

It is a lesson of our experience thus far that a great deal of time has been wasted on the sterile issue of which should come first, a treaty on general disarmament or limited measures of disarmament and arms control. It should be apparent that whichever is practically feasible should come first. Which this is can only be discovered by face-to-face exploration of specific proposals. It stands to reason that simpler measures which involve less adjustment, fewer concessions, and a minimum of domestic problems in the states concerned will usually be more readily acceptable and comparatively easier to work out. Therefore limited measures of disarmament and arms control should receive the greater immediate emphasis. In spite of appearances, this is what has happened at Geneva, especially after the agreements of 1963. Thus, although Soviet representatives still inveigh against "arms control without disarmament" and proclaim a strong preference for "general and complete disarmament first," in actual fact they have been discussing and proposing limited measures for quite some time. It is on such measures that we should in the immediate future be putting our strongest effort, always bearing in mind that the limited steps may be the building blocks for an eventually far more comprehensive structure.

Finally, as was said earlier, it is not logical to expect a major reduction of arms or even total disarmament alone to bring with it an absence of conflict. Although there is much misunderstanding and wishful thinking on this point, it is clear that one cannot expect the unavailability of certain weapons to change the nature of man. Just as Cain slew Abel, as long as there is greed and ambition, so long will men and nations be tempted to take what is not theirs. As long as there is injustice, whether fancied or real, so long will men be tempted to take by force what they feel rightly belongs to them. In such a situation the absence of arms will merely amount to the removal of *one* means of influencing the conduct of other states. Some states will still remain bigger than others, wealthier, with better natural resources, industrially more developed, and with a larger or better-trained population, a larger "internal police force," more sophisticated nuclear "know-how," and a more advantageous geographic location. Though the list could be continued, it should be sufficient to show that vast opportunities for political blackmail and coercion will continue to exist. In other words, in the absence of arms, equations of political force will be drawn in different terms but they will still be drawn. It follows that it will be essential to provide both a disarming and a disarmed world with international peace-keeping forces that are appropriately financed and staffed and, above all, effective. Just how this can be done has not yet been answered; the problem of enforcement, as we saw in the Congo and elsewhere, raises issues on which we can now see no way to agreement. But it must be done if significant disarmament is to be anything more than a dream.

The quest for disarmament should be relentlessly pursued. Nevertheless, it is impossible to escape the conclusion from all the foregoing considerations that it is vain to expect rapid progress toward general and complete disarmament. The conclusion flows from the nature of the subject itself and from the basic differences in the goals which the United States, the Soviet Union, and Communist China (not to mention France and other states with strikingly independent policies) seek to achieve.

What Disarmament Requires

Disarmament is a supremely complicated subject of Gargantuan proportions. We have noted its inseparable relationship with national defense and military power. Among the difficulties in arriving at an equitable formula for reducing armed strength is the problem of balancing the various elements of a particular nation's power against those of another. The United States, for example, is primarily a sea and air power; the Soviet Union is a land-oriented continental power with growing naval and fishing fleets. What is the balance between one nation's tanks against another's aircraft carriers and nuclear-powered submarines, or between intermediate-range missiles on one side and intercontinental ballistic missiles on the other? Even if there were no cold war in Europe but a condition of "peaceful engagement"[3] and the negotiating nations were on friendly terms, there would still be the problem of balancing out the differences among them. These would involve, in addition to arms themselves, the impact of the domestic political system on the successful implementation of disarmament agreements, geographic location, strategic doctrine and problems, industrial production and potential, educational levels and the availability of highly trained personnel, reliance on foreign trade and raw materials, and a host of other factors. It is almost impossible to compare these elements in a meaningful way, but the relative positions on all such levels would affect the impact of a particular disarmament agreement on each of the nations involved. These problems, which were very prominent in the interwar disarmament discussions, have acquired a new dimension with the development of postwar weaponry and the achievements in space.

In addition, we have only begun to take the measure of problems which are new to our times, at least in their urgent form. There are, for example, the particularly perplexing problems involved in deciding on the powers to be given to the peace-keeping institutions that will be necessary in a disarming and disarmed world. In the exchanges at Geneva on the nature of the international force required to keep the peace, the Soviet representatives have argued for national internal police forces

[3] For an exposition of "peaceful engagement" in Europe, see Zbigniew Brzezinski, *Alternative to Partition: For a Broader Conception of America's Role in Europe* (New York: McGraw-Hill, for the Council on Foreign Relations, 1965).

equipped with small non-nuclear arms of various types, which would be called into international service by the Security Council if necessary. The American position has been that a standing international force should be created and that it might have to be equipped with nuclear weapons against the contingency that some state illegally retains such weapons and breaks the peace after the supposed completion of total disarmament. The matter is far from settled and indeed raises the most far-reaching questions.

If, as the U.S. draft outline of 1962 put it, the international force is to be strong enough "effectively to deter or suppress any threat or use of arms," then it must itself be more powerful than any combination that might be raised against it. If it is to be that powerful, how is it to be kept from becoming the most powerful organization in the world? Who is to control it? The Security Council, with the veto power intact? The General Assembly, with its 117 or more disparate members? The Secretary-General, without reference to the country from which he comes, the United Nations body to which he responds, or whoever pays the costs?

Or is the proposal for an effective international peace-keeping force, logically speaking, another way of urging world government? If this is so, and if the conditions for such world government do not exist, is it possible to have general and complete disarmament? Or must we be content for the time being with some halfway measures of limited disarmament and with limited peace-keeping forces, whose primary functions would be to keep the great powers out of conflicts in which their vital interests are not involved? It cannot be said that the United States or any other nation sees its way clearly in this problem. Nor have we even begun to probe deeply into a number of others, both general and technical, such as the difficulties of verifying the limitation or elimination of bacteriological and chemical warfare.

These differences and difficulties are very important. But they might conceivably be amenable to resolution if there were sufficient political consensus between the United States and the Soviet Union. Indeed, it has in some instances become fashionable to explain the lack of agreement on disarmament by a theory of the "built-in joker," i.e., that both the United States and the Soviet Union deliberately include in their proposals so-called jokers which they know in advance will not be acceptable to the other side. Thus, according to this theory, each side is merely going through certain meaningless motions, and the entire disarmament discussion becomes nothing but a farce. This is an inaccurate oversimplification, and indeed a shocking distortion, of what has been going on in Geneva and elsewhere. No, the record of disagreement is not to be explained in these cynical Machiavellian terms. Rather it is a reflection of basic differences on world goals and therefore much more difficult. As President Kennedy expressed it after his chilling meeting with Premier Khrushchev in Vienna in 1961, "We have wholly different concepts of where the world is and where it is going."[4]

The disarmament discussions became primarily explorations of these differences and of what common ground might exist in spite of them. Let us consider briefly some of the points which came to the fore in those talks, concentrating on the ways in which the two sides looked at the "how" of disarmament.

Divergent Soviet and American Views

On the matter of sovereignty the Soviet draft treaty, not surprisingly, places its emphasis on a strictly defined, highly traditional, inviolable concept of state sovereignty. Accordingly, it does not provide for any central peace-keeping authority but calls instead for the use of internal police forces under Article 43 of the UN Charter and under the control of the Security Council. It further seeks to insure national control by providing that command of the national units to be provided under Article 43 should be made up on the "troika" formula, of "representatives of the three principal groups of States existing in the world [capitalist, Communist, and nonaligned] on the basis of equal representation."[5]

[4] Richard P. Stebbins, ed., *Documents on American Foreign Relations, 1961,* (New York: Harper & Row, for the Council on Foreign Relations, 1962), p. 91.
[5] Soviet Draft Treaty, Article 37, *Documents on American Foreign Relations, 1962,* cited, p. 110.

Unhampered by the great weight of suspicion and secrecy which the Soviet Union carries, the United States and Great Britain have tried to go beyond such a confining and unsatisfactory approach to deal with the real problem of how to organize the peace. They have tried to work out concrete measures toward the development of new institutions which would be adequate to the tasks that would confront them in a disarming and eventually disarmed world. Their efforts are still exploratory, but at least they do represent honest attempts to push aside present obstacles to effective solutions. This is only one example of persistent differences in conceptual approach.

The Soviet draft shows an impatient drive for measures which would immediately put the West at a military disadvantage, while the U.S. draft outline concentrates on a slower process of proportionate reduction of arms, coupled with the careful development of adequate institutions for the settlement of disputes and for peaceful change. As we shall see below, the Soviet draft treaty, with slight modifications by Foreign Minister Gromyko in 1962 and 1963 and by Ambassador Tsarapkin in Geneva in February of 1964, provides for the immediate destruction of practically all nuclear weapon delivery vehicles (though not of the nuclear warheads themselves) in Stage I of disarmament and the immediate abandonment of all military bases, troop deployment, and missile sites maintained by one country on the territory of another country. It provides also for the prohibition of all joint maneuvers and for the establishment of denuclearized zones (including the territory of West Germany but no part of the Soviet Union). All these measures would have the effect of breaking down the military effectiveness of NATO while leaving Soviet defenses intact on its own vast geographical territory.

Furthermore, the Soviet government insisted, and continues to insist, that its proposals be accepted "in principle" before its representatives will consent to the discussion of what they call "details," such as timing, inspection, verification, and how many and what kinds of weapons would be involved. In contemplating these aims, it is indeed hard to escape the conclusion that the Soviet Union has, as my predecessor in Geneva, Ambassador James J. Wadsworth, put it, used arms control negotiations as "part of a grand strategy aimed at the eventual total defeat of the other side."[6]

The Western nations, while mindful of the need to approach the problems in terms of their own security and world outlook, have nevertheless tried to devise proposals which are also responsive to legitimate Soviet concern for security. In spite of differences in detail, the United States and Great Britain have been in general agreement as to how the goal of disarmament might be accomplished: through a balanced reduction of arms, to be carried out in fixed proportions during three stages, with verification at each stage.[7] As I put it before the ENDC on April 18, 1962, since a tolerable balance of forces existed in the world at that moment, "the nations of the world should seize a moment in time to stop the arms race, to freeze the military situation as it then appears and to shrink it progressively to zero, always keeping the relative military position of the parties to the treaty as near as possible to what it was at the beginning."[8] This idea of balance had already been expressed in the Joint Statement of Agreed Principles of September 20, 1961, which had put it in the following way:

> All measures of general and complete disarmament should be balanced so that at no stage of the implementation of the treaty could any State or group of States gain military advantage and that security is ensured equally for all.[9]

This balanced disarmament was to be accompanied by: (1) a system of international inspection adequate to report any violations, including those that related to excessive levels of armaments retained illegally in contravention of the quantities authorized for that phase of the disarmament process; and (2) the simultaneous and pioneering development of stronger international institutions for keeping the peace and for insuring that all change would be peaceful, to the point, as Secretary of State

[6] *The Price of Peace* (New York: Praeger, 1962), p. 21.

[7] Sir Michael Wright, *Disarm and Verify* (London: Chatto and Windus; New York: Praeger; 1964), especially Chs. 10, 11, 13.

[8] United States Arms Control and Disarmament Agency, *Documents on Disarmament, 1962,* v. I (Washington: GPO, 1963), p. 384.

[9] Stebbins, *Documents on American Foreign Relations, 1961,* cited, p. 202.

Herter had said in 1960, "where aggression will be deterred by international rather than national force."[10]

The keynotes of the Western draft are gradual and peaceful change, maintenance of the existing balance, open reassurance, and international peace-keeping. The keynotes of the Soviet draft are disruption of the existing balance, secrecy, reliance on verification largely under national management, and the big-power veto in the Security Council on peace-keeping. We must persist, but it is hard to find a meeting ground between these opposing views.

The Issue of Delivery Vehicles

Let us take the comparison a little further by examining one aspect of the Soviet and American draft proposals, dealing with the central question of how to liquidate delivery vehicles for nuclear weapons. The United States, in its 1962 draft, dealt with these vehicles as part of a general provision for an across-the-board, carefully phased and implemented, progressively larger percentage reduction of military hardware, which would, as we saw it, best serve the aims of disarmament and general security, while at the same time disturbing the existing balance the least. We therefore provided for a 30 per cent reduction in both conventional and nuclear armaments in Stage I, to be taken in equal installments during the three years of that stage, plus a stated reduction in conventional armed forces. The Soviet draft, in contrast, called for the immediate abolition of all foreign military bases and, originally, for the immediate destruction of all nuclear weapon delivery systems,[11] as had first been proposed by Jules Moch, the French delegate, in 1959. The elimination of the nuclear weapons themselves was reserved for Stage II.

The Soviet draft treaty was and remains unacceptable to the

[10] Speech of February 18, 1960, in Richard P. Stebbins, ed., *Documents on American Foreign Relations, 1960* (New York: Harper & Row, for the Council on Foreign Relations, 1961), p. 189.

[11] Though originally no percentage reduction had been provided, on July 16, 1962, the Soviet representative announced a decision to amend the proposal by applying a 30 per cent reduction to conventional armaments, but to them alone. There was also provision in the Soviet draft for the reduction of armed forces in Stage I.

United States and to Great Britain. As we put it at the time, it was not a true plan for disarmament but rather a plan to disarm the free world. It would virtually have forced the United States to give up at the start those arms on which it had placed a heavy reliance for the defense of itself and its allies, and in which, as a sea and air power, it had marked superiority. The plan would have forced the withdrawal of the United States from a number of overseas bases and gravely weakened its alliances. The result would have been to give a major advantage to the Soviet Union, with its vast land area stretching from Europe to the Kamchatka Peninsula in the Pacific and from the Arctic Circle to the Black Sea, with its contiguous relationship to its allies, and with its preponderance in manpower and conventional weapons. Statistical comparisons of Soviet power with that of all the countries in NATO are largely meaningless.

These Soviet proposals have not been significantly amended. For a while there seemed to be a glimmer of hope that some compromise suggestion on the immediate destruction of delivery vehicles might be in the making, when Foreign Minister Andrei Gromyko proposed at the General Assembly in September 1962 that in the process of destroying vehicles for the delivery of nuclear weapons during the first stage "exception be made for a strictly limited and agreed number of global intercontinental missiles, anti-missile missiles and anti-aircraft missiles of the ground-to-air type," which each nuclear power could keep, exclusively on its own territory, until the end of the second stage.[12]

A year later Mr. Gromyko told the same body that "limited contingents of intercontinental, anti-missile and anti-aircraft missiles should remain at the disposal of the Soviet Union and the United States in their own territories . . . until the end of the third stage," that is, until the end of the disarmament process.[13] In February 1964 Mr. Tsarapkin indicated that as part of the

[12] GAOR, 17th Sess., 1127th Plenary Meeting, September 21, 1962, *Documents on Disarmament, 1962,* cited, v. II, pp. 904-905. This change applies only to Article 5 of the Soviet draft treaty as revised on September 22, 1962. For text, see *Documents on American Foreign Relations, 1962,* cited, pp. 173-176.

[13] GAOR, 18th Sess., 1208th Plenary Meeting, September 19, 1963, *Documents on Disarmament, 1963* (Washington: GPO, 1964) p. 516.

proposed "nuclear umbrella" the two powers should retain the following: (1) intercontinental ballistic missiles, (2) antimissile missiles, and (3) antiaircraft missiles in the "ground-to-air" category. All of these would be located on Soviet and United States territory only and under "strict control" at the launching pads.[14] No further explanation has been offered.

It is clear from this brief summary that the hopeful estimates of the significance of Gromyko's 1962 statement were misplaced. There has been no forward movement. We have made numerous efforts to find out just what the Soviet government had in mind, to bring the discussion down to concrete details, to find out how many delivery vehicles would be included in the proposed "nuclear umbrella," and to ascertain how the desired end might then be verified effectively. We have met with a blanket refusal to go beyond the "either-or" demand that we either accept the idea "in principle" or not discuss it at all. Since we obviously cannot accept such a one-sided proposal "in principle," there has been no progress on this crucial topic.

It may be worthwhile at this point to take cognizance of the argument so often advanced by the Soviet Union that the U.S. draft outline does not, *in Stage I,* provide guarantees against nuclear war, whereas the Soviet proposal for the elimination (or virtual elimination) of nuclear delivery vehicles does. The fact of the matter is that there is a broad "twilight zone" in which it is factually impossible to draw the distinction between vehicles which are "capable" of delivering nuclear weapons and those which are not.[15] The Soviet draft (Articles 5 [4] and 15) specifically allows for the production of rockets subjectively characterized as being for "peaceful purposes." In addition, it should be pointed out that a number of vehicles which are not designed to carry nuclear weapons could be converted to do so, as the Communist Chinese apparently did in detonating their second nuclear explosion.

Thus, in order to achieve the Soviet claim of a guarantee

[14] Speech in Plenary Session, February 4, 1964, in ENDC. *Further Documents Relating to the Conference of the Eighteen-Nation Committee on Disarmament,* Cmd. 2486 (London: H.M.S.O., 1964), pp. 56-57.
[15] The significance of this point in relation to Communist China's atomic explosions is discussed below (see pp. 128-130).

against nuclear war in Stage I, the Soviet draft would have to provide for the elimination of every vehicle which *could* carry a nuclear weapon. This definition would include a large number of conventional aircraft, submarines, and surface warships. But the Soviet draft, as amended in Article 11 (3), proposes only to reduce military conventional aircraft by 30 per cent during the first stage and does not deal with other conventional aircraft at all. This brief statement, given by way of example only, serves as the merest indication of the imprecision and the dangers concealed in the Soviet draft treaty.

Enough for now of this enormous and many-sided topic, the writing of the history of which the author leaves to other hands. Perhaps it will be clear to the reader why the discussions have been so tedious and unproductive (except for clarification), and why it is so essential to continue probing Soviet intentions, as we did at the time of the Cuban missile crisis. Nevertheless, we continue to talk, because it cannot be predicted when some measure of agreement might suddenly become possible, and also because something may be learned in the process of analysis, thinking, and talking.

*　　　　*　　　　*

Exasperating and annoying as our experience with the problems of disarmament has been, it was not unexpected. There had been fifteen years of unrequited labor for other American representatives before I became involved in it. At the time I undertook the assignment, under the direction of President Kennedy and of Mr. McCloy, the decision was taken to press urgently for limited agreements and at the same time to work on the draft text of a treaty on general disarmament. I was determined to study, and attempt to meet constructively, substantive Soviet points and not to become unnecessarily irritated with Soviet tactics and the apparent pointlessness of continuing unproductive exchanges. Mere lack of agreement was not, and is not, adequate reason to discontinue the negotiations for an agreement on general disarmament.

Knowing the obstacles to such an agreement, however, we

hoped for quicker and more tangible results in the more limited field. In 1963 that hope was rewarded by the signing of three limited agreements. The first was the so-called "hot-line" accord of June 20, 1963, which provided for a direct communications link between the U.S. and Soviet governments "for use in time of emergency."[16] This agreement was a direct outgrowth of the dissatisfaction with communications during the Cuban crisis of the previous fall. The second was the partial nuclear test-ban treaty of August 5, 1963, which will be discussed in Chapter V. And the third was the Resolution Against the Placing of Nuclear Weapons in Space, approved by the General Assembly on October 17, 1963, by acclamation.[17] The existence of these agreements made it easier to go ahead in 1964 with what might be termed reciprocal steps based on a policy of "mutual example."

It will be noted that none of these agreements was actually a disarmament measure, in the sense of the immediate physical reduction or elimination of weapons. Perhaps the Resolution on Nuclear Weapons in Space may be called a measure of preventive limited disarmament. Actually, the term "limited measure" subsumes a variety of possibilities, only some of which will involve the actual liquidation of arms. One example in the latter category, proposed but never agreed upon, was a "bonfire" of obsolete manned bomber planes to be carried out by the Soviet Union and the United States under inspection.

Of perhaps even livelier interest are measures which seek to control arms rather than to reduce their actual numbers. The emphasis of arms control measures is different from that of limited disarmament, and the difference has on occasion caused some confusion. It is really quite simple. Proponents of arms control seek to increase stability and reduce the danger of war by a variety of measures resting on a recognition that, as a leading study put it,

. . . our military relation with potential enemies is not one of pure

---

[16] Richard P. Stebbins, ed., *Documents on American Foreign Relations, 1963* (New York: Harper & Row, for the Council on Foreign Relations, 1964), pp. 115-116. The "hot line," although functioning, has not yet been called into service.

[17] Same, p. 155.

conflict and opposition, but involves strong elements of mutual interest in the avoidance of a war that neither side wants, in minimizing the costs and risks of the arms competition, and in curtailing the scope and violence of war in the event it occurs.[18]

Thus arms control measures may take a variety of forms and may be unilateral or reciprocal. On the unilateral side they may involve measures to "harden" missile sites to make missiles less vulnerable and thus to reduce the pressure to fire them first, before they are ruined by enemy attack; to avoid provocative close-to-the-border flights; and to minimize the risk of war by accident through rigorously controlled procedures in the handling of nuclear weapons.

Other possibilities include mutually agreed arrangements such as the "hot-line" agreement, the exchange of information on some military matters, or steps to reduce the risk of surprise attack. In some instances arms control measures may even involve an increase in military expenditure or an increase in the production of some weapons while others may be cut back. Naturally, disarmament and arms control measures are not mutually exclusive, and U.S. proposals have, over the years, contained a "mix" of the two approaches. Some of these possibilities will be taken up in Chapter VI.

[18] T. C. Schelling and M. H. Halperin, *Strategy and Arms Control* (New York: Twentieth Century Fund, 1961), p. 1.

Chapter V

Nuclear Test-Ban Treaty

The partial test-ban treaty of August 5, 1963,[1] is noteworthy in at least two respects, one apparent and the other not so well recognized. Indisputably, the treaty marked the first breakthrough in all the years of effort since 1946 to reach some mutually satisfactory agreement with the Soviet Union on the control of nuclear weapons. Although it did not cover underground tests and required no radical concessions on the part of the Soviet Union, except, perhaps, giving up its proposal for an uninspected "moratorium" on underground testing, it did at least signal a willingness to take a first step. It was, as President Kennedy put it, "a shaft of light" in what had been a darkness of disagreement. At least one could hope that the conclusion of this agreement might lead to further forward steps between the two great nuclear powers.

On September 24, 1963, the U.S. Senate by a vote of 80 to 19, gave its consent to the partial test-ban treaty. On October 7 it was ratified by President Kennedy. At the moment of writing, 113 states have signed or acceded to the treaty, with only France, Communist China, the latter's ideological adherents, and a few others holding aloof.[2]

[1] Text in Richard P. Stebbins, ed., *Documents on American Foreign Relations, 1963* (New York: Harper & Row, for the Council on Foreign Relations, 1964), pp. 130-132.

[2] Albania, Cambodia, Communist China, Congo (Brazzaville), Cuba, France, Guinea, North Viet-Nam, North Korea, and Saudi Arabia have not signed. All 113 states signed or deposited appropriate instruments. The East German

The second noteworthy aspect is that the treaty rests on a fairly fine balance between political advantage and risk. The crux of the matter lies in the fact that there can be no absolute certainty under present conditions that, despite scientific advances, every test explosion which might take place in the prohibited environments will be detected and identified by the national methods available under the treaty. This is not to say that improvements may not take place in detection and identification methods. Certainly, our and other nations' scientists are working without interruption on the problem, which is a complicated one involving the use of far earth, solar, and outer space satellites. The treaty itself, however, is based not on what might happen in the future but on the acceptance of the risk that some test explosion in outer space, the atmosphere, or under water might pass unnoticed.

American officials charged with responsibility for the negotiations reached the conclusion that the degree of risk involved was acceptable for a number of reasons. First of all, the United States was superior to the Soviet Union in over-all military capacity, and it was felt that a test ban in the three prohibited environments would help to freeze that superiority, even if the Soviets were to improve their missiles (as they apparently have done by increasing range and by moving to the solid-fuel type). Furthermore, we felt that by outlawing testing in the three environments under a solemn treaty obligation we increased the cost, difficulty, and political risks of clandestine testing so drastically as to reduce its significant military value.

This is not to say that we relied on a misty, vague "world opinion" to deter the would-be violator. We realized well enough that the nation which will be curbed by world opinion is usually the one that least needs curbing. Furthermore, we had before us the example of the conference of the nonaligned at Belgrade in September 1961, the members of which had protested only very mildly when the Soviet Union broke the voluntary moratorium on testing that had been in effect for almost three years, and also

---

regime, the Byelorussian S.S.R., and the Ukrainian S.S.R., none of which is recognized as a separate sovereign state by the United States, signed in Moscow. The two Soviet republics are, however, members of the United Nations.

the example of the session of the UN General Assembly that year where India, a self-proclaimed "nonaligned" state, led the fight against any censure of the Soviet Union. No, it was not on an uncertain world opinion that we who favored the partial test-ban treaty relied for an inhibiting effect but on realistic calculations of where both American and Soviet national interests lay in this matter.

Although the Senate hearings on the partial test-ban treaty in August 1963 showed that this assessment of acceptable risk was a sticking point for a number of people, it was and is the conviction of those who supported the treaty that, so long as there are no drastic changes on the international scene unfavorably affecting our vital interests, the risk is in fact acceptable to the United States and is far outweighed by the treaty's advantages.

The advantages, which are primarily political, have been recited often enough. It was hoped that the patiently negotiated treaty would open the way to further agreements; reduce tensions between the United States and the Soviet Union; lead to a keener appreciation in some other countries of the U.S. commitment to sound disarmament agreements; help check the arms race; reduce radioactive fallout in the atmosphere and lessen the menace to health; inhibit the further proliferation of nuclear weapons; and take the wind out of the completely irresponsible and unintelligent propaganda campaign, including the "ban the bomb" movements, being conducted against the nuclear powers at the United Nations, in England and elsewhere.

In all these ways the partial nuclear test-ban treaty gave some promise of strengthening our security and that of other nations. These were our hopes. That is why we did not give up on the negotiations. Let me be clear: it was not emotion but patience, creativeness, imagination, and a continuing re-examination of scientific advances, plus President Kennedy's unfailing and constant support, that brought the treaty into being.

Just how the treaty in its few years of existence has contributed to the achievement of these hopes is difficult to state with any real degree of accuracy. When dealing with the many threads which go to make up the skein of history, one can speak only in relative terms. Certainly, the treaty has slowed down the further development of nuclear weapons and missiles that testing in the atmosphere would have facilitated. It has also resulted in a decrease in radioactive fallout. It is my personal opinion that, in view of the pressure from many quarters and of our own revulsion against the effects of fallout on future generations, the United States, even without the partial test-ban treaty, probably within a few years would have ceased nuclear testing in two of the three prohibited environments, leaving only outer space. Furthermore, the treaty helped to weaken those in the United States and elsewhere who were making naïve, unanchored proposals in this field.

Finally, and not least important, the very existence of the treaty helped to contribute to an emerging atmosphere of *détente* between the United States and the Soviet Union and to strengthen, at least for a while, those elements in the Soviet Union which were in favor of shaping better relations with the West. Relations have become strained, more recently, by the Viet-Nam affair, to which Moscow has reacted by denouncing U.S. military measures and by materially aiding North Viet-Nam with missiles and missile-launching sites. Yet so far, at least, the Soviets apparently have not jettisoned the line of "peaceful coexistence" with the West despite the evaporation of much of the atmosphere of *détente*. Indeed, the efforts in the Security Council in the fall of 1965 to obtain a cease-fire agreement between India and Pakistan illustrate how effectively the two great powers can work in unison through the United Nations.

Many factors, of course, including our own negotiations, entered into this trend toward better relations that developed in 1963, such as President Kennedy's correspondence with Premier Khrushchev and his speech at the American University in June; it is important, as always, not to claim too much. Historians may debate for quite some time the reasons for the Soviet decision to enter into the partial test-ban treaty after so many years of obduracy. In part, no doubt, they were willing because by limiting the prohibitions to three environments in August 1962, the West had removed those provisions, obnoxious to the Soviet Union, having to do with verification of the nature of otherwise unidentified underground seismic events. In part, there were calculations of domestic needs and pressures. And, in part, the shock of controversy both in Cuba and in the Sino-Soviet relationship may have made an agreement seem more desirable.

Whatever the combination of reasons, it is my conclusion that the nuclear test-ban treaty, by the very fact that it proved possible, helped to bring on the modest progress represented by the additional steps which took place in 1963 and 1964. Further concrete developments may still be brought about by the same type of nonpolemical, imaginative, patient negotiations.

At the time it was negotiated and ratified, the partial test-ban treaty was the center of public attention, both in the United States and elsewhere. Much of this attention was highly laudatory. There was a sense of positive achievement. Satisfaction with it, however, should not blind the American people to the importance of keeping a realistic anchor to windward. It is necessary to keep in mind what the treaty does *not* do.

It does not deal in any way with the use of nuclear weapons, their production, their quantitative limitation, or their improvement by underground testing. It has nothing to do with the design of nuclear weapons in laboratories without testing, as was the case with the bomb we dropped over Hiroshima, though it is much more difficult or risky or may even be nearly impossible to develop reliable weapons in this way. Furthermore, we should remember that the Soviets, with their belief in the triumph of world-wide communism, are not averse to trying to create an atmosphere of euphoria in the West while continuing to pursue international Communist goals basically hostile to it. In other words, the success of the nuclear test-ban treaty in our terms rests on maintaining national alertness and relative superiority in our military strength, without which we could not afford its risks.

Indeed, for the foreseeable future the very possibility of disarmament and arms control measures and their success will rest on our industrial, scientific, and military strength, and here we must recognize a problem. If we were to enter into a period of increasing *détente* with the Soviet Union (though following the fall of Khrushchev it is still difficult to see precisely where his successors stand), it may also be a period in which the pressures for not maintaining that strength may mount.

As Roswell Gilpatric, the able former Deputy Secretary of Defense, expressed it in a probing article, "The United States may face a dilemma over the extent and use of its military power in the event the cold war with the Soviet Union eases before major steps are taken toward general disarmament."[3] The issue may be posed more sharply in the event of future measures and agreements on arms control or limited disarmament.

We must not allow ourselves to resolve this dilemma in the wrong way, should we be faced with it. Enticing though the prospect of *détente* may be, we will have to remember that, for the time being at least, it must rest on our relative superiority over the Soviet Union in military and general national strength. We will also have to take into account the power needed to meet our world-wide responsibilities, which are by definition much broader than our relations with the Soviet Union per se.

At the same time, we should continue to seek agreed measures of disarmament, adjusting to the new situation they bring about. These are not contradictory policies, but, as Mr. Gilpatric put it, we will have to "keep equally alert to both the possibilities of peace and the dangers of aggression." This is a difficult task, requiring restraint, understanding, and the exercise of strong leadership.

The Course of Negotiations

The partial test-ban treaty is the end result of some five years of intensive though intermittent labor. For the United States, many were involved in it: on the negotiating side at Geneva, Ambassador Wadsworth, Charles C. Stelle, the author, David Popper, Ronald Spiers, Lawrence Weiler, David Mark, and Alex Akalovsky, with the invaluable support of Presidents Eisenhower and Kennedy, Secretaries of State Dulles, Herter, and Rusk, Under Secretary of State Harriman, John J. McCloy, William C. Foster, Adrian S. Fisher, Carl Kaysen, William Tyler, and John T. McNaughton.

For Great Britain, Prime Minister Macmillan, Lord Home, Sir David Ormsby-Gore (now Lord Harlech), Sir Michael Wright,

---

[3] "Our Defense Needs: The Long View," *Foreign Affairs*, April 1964, p. 366.

and later Joseph Godber and Lord Hailsham (Quintin Hogg) were the principal negotiators.

All toiled unstintingly through these marathon negotiations without any assurance that there would ever be a treaty at the end of the road.

I would like at this point to pay tribute to the truly great work of the American scientists who participated in these negotiations. In 1958 at the Conference of Experts to Study the Possibility of Detecting Violations of a Possible Agreement on Suspension of Nuclear Tests—to give the full title of the meetings—and in subsequent years they set up with infinite care and thoroughness the proposed system of detecting and identifying nuclear explosions in various environments. James B. Fisk, chairman of the initial American delegation of experts, Hans Bethe, George B. Kistiakowsky, Frank Press, Jerome B. Wiesner, Wolfgang Panofsky, Spurgeon Keeney, and Herbert Scoville were among the many able scientists who made invaluable contributions.

These five years of negotiation, which began at the time of the unilateral moratoria on nuclear weapons testing in 1958, moved through a tangle of proposals for both comprehensive and partial test bans. At times the matter was considered separately, at times it was enmeshed in the discussions on general disarmament. By the end of 1960 it was hard to know how to draw the balance. On the one hand, agreement had been reached on a preamble, seventeen articles, and two annexes of a draft treaty for a comprehensive test ban, including one article which recognized the principle of international inspection. On the other hand, the diplomatic atmosphere had deteriorated markedly since the collapse of the summit conference in May 1960 after the U-2 incident.

After President Kennedy's inauguration a new emphasis was placed on achieving a comprehensive nuclear test-ban treaty. The matter was carefully considered within the government. Secretary of Defense McNamara gave his blessing. Our military leaders, the Atomic Energy Commission, and the members of the Joint House and Senate Committee on Atomic Energy were naturally and professionally cautious, placing heavy emphasis on the need for the unrestricted development of nuclear weapons in relation to the Soviet Union and citing the utility of unhampered nuclear explosions for peaceful purposes. There were also some scientists who took the same view or feared that a test ban might lead to the closing down of the big laboratories necessary for continuing nuclear research.

The State Department and other political advisers, while keenly aware of the need for maintaining the armed strength of the United States, saw the problem more strongly in terms of political advantage, combined with a realization that changing nuclear strategies made the all-out development of new nuclear weapon types less crucial than a few years earlier. The President ultimately decided, in part on the basis of the report in February-March 1961 of a special committee under Dr. Fisk, and after a favorable recommendation by the National Security Council, that it would be to our national advantage to work for a comprehensive test-ban treaty.

This decision, incidentally, provided a good illustration of President Kennedy's attitude toward the role of science in the making of governmental policy. He knew the value of the best scientific advice, which he got from his own adviser, Dr. Jerome Wiesner, and from many other able scientists. The President was well aware of the need for the most intensive and creative scientific research if our political decisions and policies were to be sound. He deeply respected scientists, liked them, and encouraged them. He declined, however, to permit scientists in effect to make political decisions by accepting as final their word as to how the future would be. Like Sir Winston Churchill, he was forever reading, criticizing, querying, prodding, asking, in an effort to push scientific frontiers wider, to ferret out new approaches and methods which might make political goals more feasible. He knew that the one who held political responsibility had to take the final decisions on high policy on the basis of many considerations, tangible and intangible, other than the purely scientific.

With this mixed background of determination at home and a somewhat unpromising international situation, we began in 1961, with President Kennedy's full support, what were to be two years of hard, unrelenting, intensive, interesting, and challenging work. Consulting often with our own and British scientists, we missed no opportunity to discuss the test ban with Soviet representatives, on and off the record, whether at Geneva, at the United Nations, or in private diplomatic conversations which went on continuously. In spite of a solid wall of Soviet negatives, we kept on trying to adjust our proposals as science and political developments made changes possible. We were convinced of the importance of our goal, and we knew that after careful and persistent preparation agreement with the Soviet Union could come suddenly and without warning, as had been the case with the Austrian State Treaty of 1955.

Personally deeply convinced that on balance a comprehensive nuclear test-ban treaty was in the interests of the United States and would encourage the reduction of tensions in the world, my colleagues and I bent every effort, night and day, day in and day out, to discharge a double duty: daily to review our position with our scientists and to present as forcefully and exactly as possible the joint U.S.-U.K. position at the diplomatic table, and to seek to discover and understand fully the details of the Soviet position as a basis for our own further discussion in Washington and for the further shaping of our policy.

We had to take in stride the consistent lack of interest with which the Soviet representatives met our every proposal, amendment, and adjustment, and the unfailingly negative way in which they "set the stage" on which the Western proposals were to be presented. Thus, it was against the background of Mr. Tsarapkin's reintroduction on March 21, 1961, of the "troika" concept, based on the equality (and veto power) of Communist, Western, and neutral interests, that we presented, on April 18, 1961, without discouragement or evidence of setback, our first complete draft of a comprehensive nuclear test-ban treaty in all environments. In this draft we met most of the Soviet objections that had any legitimate basis. And it was against this background that we continued to explore and discuss the test ban in every way we could and to make further proposals.

The reason for the negative Soviet position was made stunningly clear on August 30, 1961. Khrushchev had declared on earlier occasions that the first country to break a moratorium on nuclear weapons testing would take upon itself an enormous moral and political responsibility and expose itself in the eyes of all nations.[4] Now, in 1961, the Soviet government itself assumed that responsibility by announcing that it would resume nuclear weapons testing. The text of the statement and the rapidity with which the tests followed revealed that the talks had been deliberately misused as a screen for test preparations—a situation which we had begun to suspect early in the spring of 1961. We persevered in our efforts in spite of this action; on September 3, 1961, President Kennedy and Prime Minister Macmillan joined in calling upon the Soviet Union to cease further atmospheric testing, to accept a treaty barring such tests without any international controls, and to return to the discussion table to work out a comprehensive treaty. On September 9, 1961, Premier Khrushchev categorically refused.[5] Our ears were assailed that fall with the reverberations of continued Soviet testing, which the UN General Assembly only "noted with regret," as Krishna Menon of India did his best to prevent any criticism of the Soviet Union's flagrant violation of the moratorium.

By mid-1962 it seemed clear to me that the Soviet Union would not accept any proposals that involved on-site inspection of otherwise unidentifiable underground events by foreigners, no matter how carefully regulated and safeguarded. Accordingly, the U.S. delegation recommended that consideration should be given to a test-ban treaty which would not cover tests carried out underground, the one environment in which we regarded such inspection as absolutely essential. President Eisenhower had in 1959 proposed such a partial ban, which had foundered on Soviet opposition. Washington now authorized our delegation to proceed on that basis. In due course, on August 27, 1962, as chairman of the American delegation, I tabled at Geneva two draft treaties, one a partial and one a comprehensive ban, and said we were prepared to sign the partial test-ban treaty in the three

[4] Letter to President Eisenhower, April 22, 1958, in Department of State, *Documents on Disarmament, 1945-1959*, v. II (Washington: GPO, 1960), p. 999; Address to the Supreme Soviet, January 14, 1960, in *Documents on Disarmament, 1960* (Washington: GPO, 1961), p. 7.

[5] Richard P. Stebbins, ed., *Documents on American Foreign Relations, 1961* (New York: Harper & Row, for the Council on Foreign Relations, 1962), pp. 183-186.

environments without inspection or the comprehensive test-ban treaty in all four with carefully worked-out inspection of otherwise unidentified underground seismic events.[6]

These drafts seemed to arouse considerable informal interest among Soviet representatives at Geneva and at the United Nations in 1962 before the Cuban crisis. This was in contrast to the official denunciation and the counterproposal for a moratorium on underground testing, which would not be prohibited by a partial test-ban treaty. But there were no positive results until the matter was taken up at the highest political levels. The private correspondence on the subject between President Kennedy and Premier Khrushchev, begun during the Cuban crisis, the public appeal of the President and Prime Minister Macmillan to the Soviet leader on April 24, 1963, the Dodd-Humphrey resolution in the Senate on May 27, 1963, and high-level diplomatic conversations all played their part in setting the stage.

On June 10, 1963, in his famous American University speech, President Kennedy announced that agreement had been reached to start three-power talks shortly in Moscow, "looking toward early agreement on a comprehensive test-ban treaty." He also stated that, in order to make clear our good faith and solemn convictions, the United States would not again conduct nuclear tests in the atmosphere so long as other states did not do so. "We will not be the first to resume," he said.

These remarks are believed to have made a profound impression on certain elements of Soviet leadership. Several weeks later, speaking in East Berlin on July 2, 1963, Premier Khrushchev made his reply. Although he decisively rejected a comprehensive test-ban treaty with on-site inspection as "legalized espionage," he dropped the earlier Soviet insistence on an unverified moratorium on underground tests and for the first time announced in public that a partial nuclear test-ban treaty in the three other environments only—outer space, the atmosphere, and under water—with the use of existing national verification systems, would be satisfactory to the Soviet government. On July 15, 1963, the further talks on a partial test-ban treaty began in Moscow, with Under Secretary Harriman as the principal negoti-

[6] United States Arms Control and Disarmament Agency, *Documents on Disarmament, 1962,* v. II (Washington: GPO, 1963), pp. 792-807.

ator for the United States, and Adrian S. Fisher, Deputy Director of the Arms Control and Disarmament Agency, as his adviser.[7]

They began in an atmosphere which could be described as promising. The so-called "hot-line" agreement on direct communications at the "heads of government" level between the United States and the Soviet Union had been reached at Geneva in June 1963. Discussions between United States and Soviet scientists on the peaceful uses of atomic energy had been resumed in May. The Soviet Union had stopped jamming Voice of America broadcasts. And the Sino-Soviet dispute, in which the Soviet Union no doubt felt pressed to "show" that its interpretation of the correct way to deal with the West would work, was rapidly developing. It may be recalled that at the very time the test-ban treaty was being negotiated a Chinese Communist delegation was in Moscow for direct talks with Soviet leaders on the Sino-Soviet split. These talks failed totally.

The treaty was formally signed in Moscow on August 5, 1963, by the Foreign Ministers of the United States, Great Britain, and the U.S.S.R. I was unofficially present at the signing, thanks to a courteous and never-to-be-forgotten telephoned invitation to Mrs. Dean and myself from President Kennedy, who remarked, "After all, it is your treaty."

Sticking Points

A reading of the day-by-day test-ban talks over the five years of their duration reveals a long and involved tale which can, however, be boiled down to rather simple terms. On the part of the Soviet Union there was a double effort: to convince the world that it desired a test ban, yet at the same time to stave off all proposals that went beyond purely national means for detection and identification of otherwise unidentified events. There were many variations on the theme, but this is what they all amounted

---

[7] For Khrushchev's reply see ACDA, *Documents on Disarmament, 1963* (Washington: GPO, 1964), pp. 244-246; on the Moscow negotiations see Arthur M. Schlesinger, Jr., *A Thousand Days: John F. Kennedy in the White House* (Boston: Houghton Mifflin, 1965), pp. 902-909.

to on close examination. The Western position, on the other hand, was characterized by movement and a consistent effort to meet Soviet objections as far as our security and the progress of science made possible.[8]

Any number of illustrative examples can be plucked from the discussions as they took place in 1961 and 1962. Take the question of the "treaty threshold," the exclusion from the treaty of underground nuclear explosions below a certain size or yield because of the usual inability of distant instrumentation to detect and identify the cause—man-made or natural—of underground events equivalent to less than 4.75 on the seismographic magnitude scale.[9] Because the Soviet Union had not wished to accept a treaty in which all such lesser underground events would be subject to on-site inspection of suspicious areas, we had in February 1960 proposed that the test-ban treaty initially not attempt to cover these seismic events of smaller yields. We also stated, however, that such a treaty might cover the smaller events later if an intensive program of seismic research, then to be instituted, yielded advances in detection and identification techniques.

In March 1960 the Soviet Union appeared to agree to this, provided that the United States, Great Britain, and the U.S.S.R. all pledged that they would not actually conduct any nuclear tests below the 4.75 "threshold" during the research period. For the next seventeen months the U.S.S.R. tried to evade the implications of its commitment to a limited moratorium on below-threshold tests by claiming that it had to be continuous up to the time when the treaty might be amended to become a comprehensive ban on all yields. Its representative professed to see in any terms less stringent than the Soviet proposal a device that would make it possible for the West to resume underground testing on yields below the threshold when the moratorium expired.

---

[8] For a discussion, see Harold K. Jacobson and Eric Stein, *Diplomats, Scientists and Politicians: The United States and the Nuclear Test Ban Negotiations* (Ann Arbor: Atomic Energy Research Project, University of Michigan Law School, 1965), 3 vols (preprint).

[9] A seismic event of 4.75 magnitude was presumed to be equivalent to an underground explosion with a yield of about 19 kilotons, in the kind of geological formation known as "tuff."

To counter this Soviet obfuscation of its March 1960 agreement, we indicated on August 28, 1961, (only two days, as it turned out, before the Soviet Union resumed testing) that the United States was "ready and prepared to negotiate here and now" for the immediate lowering or even removal of the treaty threshold, provided that the Soviet Union proved itself ready to "explore with us and open-mindedly consider those improvements or adjustments in the control system which could so increase its scientific capabilities from the outset as to warrant the lowering or removing of the threshold."[10] At the same time we again pressed the Soviet delegation to join with us in conducting a "large-scale seismic improvement research program underground." We ourselves were undertaking this research at great expense. The Soviet cooperation, though solicited, was nil. To this carefully reasoned and carefully worked-out scientific attempt to meet Soviet objections, the Soviet representative could reply only with talk of "espionage."

The story has many similar chapters. One involved the number and manning of control posts. As a result of pioneering seismic research, we were able in 1962 to come down from the original proposal for 180 manned control posts made by the scientists in 1958 to much less onerous, less expensive, and less "intrusive" numbers.

Intensive study had also influenced our proposals on the manning of these stations. Originally we had proposed international teams, without any host nationals, to do the job. In 1959, 1960, and again in April 1961 we suggested a "mix" of all nations including a fixed proportion (one-third) of host country nationals. In our August 1962 draft we proposed that control posts be maintained and manned by "nationals of the State in whose territory such station is located," although the international control organization would maintain supervision of the system, including the permanent stationing or periodic visits of observers at the control posts.[11] In suggesting this, we showed again our desire to reach agreement, recognition of the improvement in

[10] ACDA, *Documents on Disarmament, 1961* (Washington: GPO, 1962), p. 300.

[11] *Documents on Disarmament, 1962*, cited, v. II, pp. 797, 793.

national detection and verification instruments, and willingness to listen to suggestions for using nationally manned posts made by the so-called nonaligned members of the ENDC in their memorandum of April 1962. And in April 1963, in a Joint Anglo-American Memorandum,[12] we formally indicated our interest in exploring further the role of automated stations as a supplement to manned national detection and identification stations for unidentified events.

To cite only one more example, we tried to apply our research and our ingenuity to the particularly thorny topic of on-site inspections, especially how many and by whom. We had no "magic number." What we wanted was a means of giving our scientists a fair chance to identify detected but otherwise unidentified "suspicious underground events" so as to provide assurance that the treaty prohibition on testing was actually being carried out and our national security protected.

As Project Vela moved forward with renewed vigor, and as we re-evaluated the political factors involved, we were able to reduce the number of on-site inspections of unidentified events we felt necessary to give us this assurance. Thus we moved from our request, in February 1960, of twenty inspections a year in the Soviet Union to a sliding formula, proposed by the British and U.S. delegations on May 29, 1961, of from twelve to twenty inspections a year depending on the actual number of suspicious underground events that took place within the year, then to a U.S. proposal of eight to ten such inspections a year, on February 12, 1963. Later in 1963 we said that "possibly, under certain circumstances," we might be able to agree to as few as seven on-site inspections.[13]

The Soviet Union has consistently rejected these proposals, either refusing all inspections or pressing for a maximum of two or three per annum—not on a scientific but on a political basis. The reductions in our own figure, however, were not primarily bargaining proposals for a compromise figure; they were all made on the basis of careful calculation founded on the best scientific

---

[12] *Documents on Disarmament, 1963*, cited, pp. 141-145.
[13] *Documents on Disarmament, 1960*, cited, p. 38; same, *1961*, pp. 161-162; same, *1963*, pp. 37, 141-145.

knowledge then available of what we could do without on-site inspection by means of distant instrumentation to identify detected seismic events. It was not a reducing process that could be expected to go on indefinitely without regard to scientific knowledge just because the Soviet negotiators refused to agree, for as the number of inspections went down, the problem of positive identification of the great number of detected but unidentified events with no logarithmic threshold in the treaty increased in complexity.

We also tried to meet Soviet objections to international on-site inspection. As the result of a good deal of study and thought, we began to advance the concept of reciprocal on-site inspection, in which each nation would form teams to inspect the other. Unfortunately, no appreciable progress has been registered in this approach, the Soviet representatives refusing to discuss it in private talks in January 1963 and in the public discussions at Geneva of the Eighteen-Nation Disarmament Committee in April of that year. We have, therefore, continued to maintain, with considerable justification, that there must be some element of international inspection if there is to be public acceptance of the treaty.

On these disputed points the Soviet Union has taken a general and political decision as to the type of verification it is willing to accept, and it has asked others to accept that decision on faith. By contrast, the Western powers have attempted to make general proposals consistent with scientific facts, and they have shown willingness to modify their positions as the results of research and political change may indicate. We are willing to experiment, to study, to subject our proposals to scrutiny in the light of new data, and to make the results of our efforts known to others for their independent and objective examination. Thus we have not shrunk from putting up the money to explore scientifically whether, with the passage of years, we might find ourselves able to rely on distant instrumentation and thus to dispense entirely with human onsite inspection of detected but unidentified underground events. Science and further testing may in time simplify the problem of identification. But it is bound to remain a very complicated one.

We are, in Project Vela, engaged in the development of techniques for improving the capability to detect, locate, and identify nuclear detonations in all environments in order eventually to develop a system capable on its own of adequately monitoring a comprehensive nuclear test ban. But a responsible government can frame responsible proposals only in the light of the tested scientific information that exists, not on the basis of hypothetical advances which might or might not be made sometime in the distant future.

As of the moment of writing, some on-site inspections by human inspectors are essential to adequate monitoring of a comprehensive test-ban treaty since otherwise there can be no precise identification of any underground seismic events not otherwise identified. Although advances in seismological techniques and in the knowledge of how sound waves travel in the bowels of the earth make it possible to reduce the necessary number of both on-site inspections and manned control posts, thus hopefully increasing the chances for Soviet agreement to a comprehensive test ban, one should not leap to a conclusion that no on-site inspections for otherwise unidentified events will be needed in the future.

For some time to come, in my opinion, there will be still need for such inspection from both a scientific and a psychological or political standpoint. Although much good work is being done on the subject, it would be irresponsible to base policy in such an important field on the expectation of early, reliable results.

The Finished Treaty of August 5, 1963

Actually, the treaty is very similar to the partial test-ban draft we had proposed at Geneva on August 27, 1962.[14] There were some procedural changes relating to the formula under which a party could denounce the treaty and to the method by which a state could adhere to the treaty. The only major substantive change, however, is the absence from the 1963 text of the old

---

[14] See the author's testimony and comparison of the two drafts in *Nuclear Test Ban Treaty*, Hearings before Senate Committee on Foreign Relations, 88th Cong., 1st sess. (Washington: GPO, 1963), pp. 813-849.

Article II, which would have allowed nuclear test explosions for peaceful purposes in all environments, under carefully controlled circumstances, provided the original parties to the treaty agreed to them. That provision proved unacceptable to the Soviet government during the Moscow negotiations and was dropped.

Some personal views on this point may be pertinent. Underground test explosions for all purposes are allowed by the 1963 treaty provided they do not result in radioactive debris "outside the territorial limits of the State under whose jurisdiction or control such explosion is conducted." The deletion of the clause in the 1962 draft does raise questions about the feasibility of the AEC's "Plowshare" program, which would use nuclear explosives for peaceful purposes, such as the possible development of a sea-level canal in Central America.[15] On balance, however, I believe that we are better off with a total prohibition on testing in the three environments than we would have been if the original provision permitting nuclear explosions for peaceful purposes had been retained. Any nuclear explosion above ground, for whatever purpose, would result in some radioactive fallout. No matter whether a test was labeled for peaceful or nonpeaceful purposes, the scientific advances which might result could be used for military as well as nonmilitary ends. Despite the costs, it seems better, therefore, to keep the lid on as tightly as possible than to try to introduce exceptions. Besides, it is not impossible that arguments between nations as to the "subjective" purpose of a particular proposed test explosion might result in increased tensions, since any nuclear explosion will show whether a device will give a "go" or "no-go" result and will give a yield from which scientific data may be extrapolated.

The text of the treaty is not long and not complicated. It is complete, without secret annexes or binding arrangements for additional agreements to follow. Although the Soviet representatives argued strongly for some sort of commitment on the part of the United States and Great Britain to the negotiation of a nonaggression pact between the Warsaw Pact and NATO pow-

[15] See *Annual Report to Congress of the Atomic Energy Commission for 1964*, 89th Cong., 1st sess., Senate Doc. No. 8 (Washington: GPO, 1965), pp. 155-166.

ers, this maneuver led to nothing more than a promise on our part to consult with our allies on the subject. The subject is, however, likely to come up again.

The key provision of Article I states that each of the parties "undertakes to prohibit, to prevent, and not to carry out any nuclear weapon test explosions, or any other nuclear explosion, at any places under its jurisdiction or control" in the three prohibited environments. The parties also agree in the same article to refrain from causing, encouraging, or in any way participating in carrying out any nuclear test explosion anywhere in any of the three prohibited environments. In drafting these provisions it was our intent (1) to check the development of new nuclear weapons by the existing nuclear powers, and (2) to make more difficult the development, production, and acquisition of nuclear weapons by non-nuclear states. In effect, by signing the test-ban treaty, non-nuclear states have taken a small step (of varying significance according to the potential of the signatory) toward preventing the spread of nuclear weapons in the future. The possibility of acquisition by purchase, donation, or through other means still remains open, however.

In drafting the agreement we had to provide for the possibility that testing by a nonsignatory, such as France or Communist China, or violation of the agreement by a signatory power would so radically change the international situation as to undercut the basis for the treaty itself. It should be pointed out that we were thinking here of serious violations and serious changes; if the purpose of a treaty is to reduce international tensions, it should not be lightly assumed that every violation that may occur is a deliberate act calling for a denunciation of the agreement. In the event that violations of comparatively small degree do occur, they should be treated with sober responsibility and every effort made by all nations concerned to conduct an adequate investigation of intent and result.

In the event of a serious testing violation, or the development of a serious threat from outside the ranks of the signatories, the situation would of course be different. Article IV of the treaty recognizes this problem. Thus, although the treaty is of unlimited duration, it provides that each party shall "in exercising its national sovereignty" have the right to withdraw "if it decides that extraordinary events, related to the subject matter of this Treaty, have jeopardized the supreme interests of its country." It will be noted that the treaty speaks of "extraordinary events" and the placing in jeopardy of "supreme interests." As is perfectly clear from the text, it is up to each nation subjectively in its own interest to decide when such jeopardy of "supreme interests" has occurred, the treaty itself giving no guidance on this subject.

In the drafting of the treaty we were also acutely aware of the boundaries of the document with which we were dealing, i.e., that it is concerned with the testing of nuclear weapons and not with their use. Therefore the treaty does not touch on the right of self-defense, nor does it modify in any way the freedom of each signatory to react in case of attack or conflict. This question was much discussed at the hearings on the test-ban treaty before the Senate committees in August 1963, many persons expressing a fear that signatories would be fettered in their choice of weapons in the event of need. Former President Eisenhower was among those who expressed concern on this point.

The confusion appears to have arisen from a change in wording which had taken place during the Moscow negotiations in July 1963. In the draft treaty of August 1962, testing for weapons and testing for peaceful purposes had been separated into two articles.[16] It therefore made complete sense for its Article I to refer only to "nuclear weapon test explosion." However, when the treaty draft was being discussed at Moscow and it became clear that the Russians would not accept the second article dealing with peaceful explosions, we had to make an adjustment in the wording of the new Article I. As the Legal Adviser to the State Department pointed out, we could no longer accept an Article I which referred only to nuclear weapon test explosions, because such wording might make it possible for a nation to claim the right to conduct nuclear explosions in the prohibited environments on the basis that it was not a test of a weapon or that it was for peaceful purposes.[17] Therefore we had inserted in

[16] *Documents on Disarmament, 1962,* cited, v. II, p. 805.
[17] *Nuclear Test Ban Treaty,* Hearings, cited, p. 77.

Article I, after the words "nuclear weapon test explosion," the words "and other nuclear explosion." The new phrase was intended to plug a loophole, not to inhibit the freedom of choice of weapons by a nation faced with a threat to its national security. To cite an authority on treaty interpretation, "The function of the words of a treaty is to mirror [the] design" of its framers.[18] This was our design.

During the hearings there was also much discussion, both within the Senate and in the country at large, as to whether the Soviet Union can ever be considered a trustworthy treaty partner, in view of its record of treaty violations. Certainly, the drafters and the proponents of the test-ban treaty were well aware of the Soviet record. We were, however, of the opinion that the record also showed that where the Soviet Union had reached the calculation that a certain agreement was in its national interest, it kept it much as any other nation would in similar circumstances. We had reached the conclusion that the partial test-ban treaty was, in the estimation of the Soviet rulers of the time, in the Soviet national interest. For that reason we thought it likely that the Soviet Union would keep the treaty, especially if it were to be followed by a further *détente*.

At the same time we were aware that there were elements within the Soviet leadership group which had not been in favor of the test-ban treaty. We knew that the Soviet calculation of the national interest might change. We were aware of the fact that some aspects of the development of nuclear weapons could take place in laboratories without testing. For all these reasons it was my personal opinion, as expressed at the August 1963 Senate hearings and elsewhere, that a number of responsibilities were incumbent on the United States in accepting the treaty, as I believed it should. It was up to us to make as certain as possible that we had the most advanced detection and identification instruments, both new and traditional, at work in this area, without being hampered unnecessarily by budgetary limits. It was

[18] C. C. Hyde, *International Law as Interpreted and Applied by the United States*, 2nd rev. ed. (Boston: Little, Brown, 1945), v. 2, p. 1469. For a discussion of the treaty as well as related issues, see Adrian S. Fisher, "Arms Control and Disarmament in International Law," *Virginia Law Review*, November 1964, pp. 1200-1219.

imperative that we move ahead as forcefully as possible with our satellite programs and related scientific research and our Vela and space programs. In addition, it was of urgent importance that we not repeat the mistake of the 1960-61 period, as a result of which we had been unable to resume atmospheric testing until some eight months after the Soviet Union broke the moratorium in August 1961, although we were able to conduct underground tests almost immediately; that we keep up our laboratories with full complements of the best scientific personnel; that we maintain our testing tunnels and other testing facilities in operation; and that we conduct comprehensive programs of underground testing.[19] Furthermore, it was and is essential that we keep up our nuclear superiority to the extent necessary to reduce any advantage accruing to the Soviet Union from any illegal testing it might conduct. One must, to use an old-fashioned comparison, always keep the musket loaded and an alert guard at the door.

From Partial to Comprehensive Test Ban

At Geneva in September 1965 the neutrals suggested extending the partial test-ban treaty to cover underground nuclear tests yielding above 4.75 in the seismic scale of magnitude; and, pending agreement on a comprehensive treaty, a voluntary uninspected moratorium on nuclear tests below that threshold. Such an arrangement would be most difficult to enforce and would inevitably lead to many disputes over whether a particular event was above or below the threshold, since instrumentation at different geographical locations with different geological formations might record different results. The United States reiterated its desire for such a comprehensive treaty, stressing the need for adequate verification procedures, and supporting the suggestion of other nations for the exchange of scientific information among the nuclear powers as a means of promoting agreement. A comprehensive treaty covering all nuclear tests in all environments gathers particular importance if viewed as part of an effort to curb the further proliferation of nuclear weapons, which is, or

[19] See *Annual Report to Congress of the Atomic Energy Commission*, cited, pp. 63-79.

should be, one of our most urgent and poignant concerns.

It is my understanding that with its lead in nuclear power the United States could enter into a comprehensive ban without serious risk to the national security[20] and indeed that our security may benefit from a "freeze" in the testing for new weapons. Although the details of the texts would be influenced by political factors and by the state of scientific advance in which they would be negotiated, the general features of our 1962 draft, plus the already proposed combination of supplementary automated control posts inspected periodically by non-host-country nationals and some international on-site inspection of a few areas where unidentified seismic events had occurred, would most probably form a satisfactory base from our point of view. Although past experience does not indicate an enthusiastic Soviet reception, that is no reason not to define our own national goals and not to prepare unceasingly on both the scientific and political levels for further negotiations.

It would seem that chances for a comprehensive ban should improve as seismological advances overcome natural barriers to identification and cut into the actual need for on-site inspections to identify otherwise unidentifiable underground events. In 1963 we spoke of seven on-site inspections for such events on Soviet territory as being an essential minimum. However, a lesser number may become possible as the result of scientific advances which give better knowledge of the world's inner structure and of the ways in which sound travels in diverse geological formations. The research work goes on in ocean seismometers and multiple-array, deep-hole seismometer clusters. Underground tests, such as the one carried out at Amchitka Island off Alaska in October 1965, may yield significant results for the identification of earthquakes and man-made nuclear explosions. At any rate, there should be further urgent exploration of all scientific possibilities that may help to close the gap between the Soviet and U.S. positions.

There are some who feel that so little can be gained by under-

---

[20] On this point, see Secretary of Defense Robert S. McNamara's address before the Economic Club of New York, November 18, 1963, *Documents on American Foreign Relations, 1963,* cited, pp. 69-80.

ground testing that we could now take the risk of reaching a comprehensive test-ban treaty without on-site inspections.[21] On the basis of present scientific advances and what can be extrapolated from low-kiloton-yield explosions underground, I cannot quite agree with this view. It would not give us the precise assurance we need. No matter what the scientific advances, moreover, it is extremely important to keep in mind the psychological or political factors involved. Suppose that we had entered into a comprehensive test ban without any right to make on-site inspections of unidentified events. Suppose, further, that a massive underground event had taken place within the Soviet Union, about the nature of which we could not be certain, and that the Soviet authorities refused to allow any outside investigation. The reaction here, it is easy to imagine, would be one of real anxiety; and a strong feeling might easily develop that our national security required the denunciation of the comprehensive ban, especially if there was a difference of opinion among the scientists and different recordings on the various scientific instruments at different geographical locations.

It is because of the real possibility of such a development that, even if we make the hoped-for scientific progress in identification, a comprehensive test ban should provide for a small number of annual on-site inspections of otherwise unidentifiable underground events in the territory of each signatory state as a matter of right. It would not seem impossible, given a generally favorable atmosphere and the ability to rely increasingly on national means of detection and identification, for us to reach agreement with the Soviet Union on a fixed number of annual on-site inspections.

It has recently been suggested that "new improvements in national detection systems might make it possible to accept a treaty in which inspection followed a challenge based upon a threat of withdrawal. . . ."[22] If I understand this proposal correctly, what

[21] J. B. Wiesner and Herbert York, "National Security and the Nuclear Test Ban," *Scientific American,* October 1964, pp. 27-35.

[22] National Citizens' Commission, "Report of the Committee on Arms Control and Disarmament," Dr. Jerome B. Wiesner, Chairman, for presentation at the White House Conference on International Cooperation, November 28-December 1, 1965, p. 11 (mimeographed).

it means is that the parties to a comprehensive treaty banning all nuclear testing would have no absolute right to inspect otherwise unidentified seismic events, but would have the right to demand an inspection of such an event with an accompanying threat of withdrawing from the treaty if inspection was not granted.

This idea of inspection following a challenge would seem to warrant further exploration. But a previously agreed system to make the treaty work automatically without the threat of withdrawal would seem preferable. Ingenious ideas do not always work in practical political application. If experienced on-site inspection teams cannot be dispatched promptly, it may be difficult to locate the evidence of unauthorized man-made seismic events. It was for this reason that the comprehensive draft treaty submitted by the United States at Geneva on August 27, 1962, provided for a permanent staff of on-site inspection teams with adequate procedures, equipment, and training.

Of course, a comprehensive test ban, like the partial ban, would have to contain a clause providing for withdrawal for good reasons. As for nonparticipants, if such a treaty were concluded, it should be our purpose to press them hard to accede to it, to make it both economically feasible for them to join and politically costly for them not to do so.

It would be unwise to initiate formal steps on such a treaty, however, until we could be reasonably certain that the Soviet leaders wished to explore the matter realistically and were sufficiently interested in a further *détente* to make it possible to count on their carrying out such a treaty. We should need to be as sure as we could that neither they nor others around them were likely to turn round and make an arrangement with the Communist Chinese which could be damaging to our interests. Once we had some firm indications of developments, we should engage in private talks with Soviet representatives, as we have in the past, to find out quietly, without propaganda and polemics, what their interest might be in a comprehensive test ban. At that point we could see our way more clearly.

The Administration should also make as certain as possible, through consultation and the exchange of information with U.S.

Senators, especially those closely concerned with national security problems, that a comprehensive test-ban treaty would stand a fair chance of being passed in the Senate. It would be unfortunate if we were to propose a treaty, discuss it, and finally negotiate it, only to find our own Senate unwilling to give its consent. As of the moment of writing, there might be a good deal of opposition among Senators, including some who supported the partial test ban because they were reassured by the provision for underground testing and laboratory research, as well as among certain scientists and in the military establishment.

Finally, in any discussion of a comprehensive test-ban treaty we would have to keep in mind the two important nonparticipants in the treaty of 1963, France and Communist China, in view of their intention to continue testing. For the time being, our relative strength vis-à-vis the other nuclear countries is such that a comprehensive test-ban treaty would be to our advantage. But if France and Communist China or others went on with tests, we would have to be very watchful to make sure that our position did not deteriorate relatively because of our ceasing to test. Our continuing nuclear superiority can by no means be automatically assured. It will require constant attention, adequate funds, and support for intensive research efforts.

Chapter VI

Points of Emphasis

Honest and constructive efforts toward disarmament face a hard, sober, but not hopeless future. Much will depend on the political environment and on the relations between the great powers in matters other than disarmament. We have seen how the whole international scene can change under the impact of developments in the Western alliance, in Soviet-Chinese relations, or in South and Southeast Asia. But uncertainty over the future is no reason to abandon the initiative in this field. It is a matter of choosing the right points of emphasis within what is a wide and often forbidding territory. Here we need to look both at what should be done at home and at what policies we should follow in forthcoming international negotiations.

To take certain aspects of our domestic outlook first. General and complete disarmament in a peaceful world is a goal of the U.S. government. Cynics dismiss it contemptuously. It may seem so remote as not to be worth thinking about. Yet if the United States is to continue negotiating, it must have the soundest possible basis for its proposals. Therefore we need to make ourselves more ready for the approach of the conditions of a disarming and disarmed world than we now are. In part, this is a question of further study and planning in a number of different subjects.

The draft outline of a disarmament treaty which the United States submitted at Geneva on April 18, 1962, is based on the development of international peace-keeping organs and of accepted procedures for peaceful change. But we have not, within our government, really faced up to the difficult problems involved, problems to which history can give us no positive key. Do we or do we not decide to retain the veto of the permanent members of the United Nations? Who in the United Nations should determine when peace-keeping forces can be used against a violator of a disarmament treaty, or the make-up of those forces? What has been our appraisal of the United Nations peace-keeping forces in the Congo and elsewhere, especially as related to the question of keeping the peace while nations disarm?[1] How should we try to reconcile the demands for peaceful change with the rights enshrined in the concept of sovereignty? Perhaps it is not possible to answer these questions in detail so far ahead of time, but we should be devoting much thoughtful attention to them.

In the meantime, the rudimentary peace-keeping machinery of the United Nations already exists. Can it be developed into what is needed to make disarmament work? Can we expect cooperation in this task from the U.S.S.R. and France, which have been unwilling to pay for important peace-keeping activities voted by the General Assembly? Certainly, the United States should continue to support financially the peace-keeping activities of the United Nations, to back the "earmarking" of national forces for that purpose, and to make earnest and consistent efforts to devise a workable procedure for the authorization of the use of UN forces. We should give a sympathetic hearing to proposals for more effective UN peace-keeping arrangements, such as those which have been made by Frank Aiken of Ireland. But what has been done thus far represents no more than a beginning.

We should also be more active in planning to meet the possible economic consequences of disarmament. Although it seems generally agreed that it will be possible to handle the economic consequences without disastrous results,[2] it should nevertheless

[1] The excellent book of Ernest W. Lefever *Crisis in the Congo: A United Nations Force in Action* (Washington: Brookings Institution, 1965) illustrates the great limitations on UN authority even in such restricted operations as those in the Congo, a far cry from the requirements of enforcing disarmament and keeping world peace.

[2] See "United States Report to the United Nations: Economic and Social Consequences of Disarmament," in United States Arms Control and Disarmament Agency, *Documents on Disarmament, 1962,* v. II (Washington: GPO, 1963), pp. 217-275; also United Nations, *Economic and Social Consequences of Disarmament,* E/3593, February 28, 1962.

be recognized, and made clear to the public, that the process must be thoroughly planned in advance. The fact is that the economic health of certain parts of the United States is almost wholly dependent on defense contracts. In order to keep concern for these areas and their inhabitants from becoming a drag on disarmament efforts, we should encourage more than we have hitherto the drawing up of detailed alternative plans by defense industries themselves, as well as by the government and by other private groups. It is not enough to say that the economy will absorb the effects of a slowdown or cessation of military production as it did after the end of World War II. As a recent government report phrased it,

> The resources set free would, in fact, have to be effectively transferred to civilian production, rather than wasted in the form of unemployment and underutilization of plant capacity or kept busy only in make-work projects. If the transition were poorly managed, we could not only lose the use of the resources released from defense but also, through the reduction of incomes and purchasing power, lose the services of other resources now used in producing purely civilian goods and services. But there is no need for this to happen. With appropriate public and private policies, a reduction of the defense budget can and should be a source of increased material welfare for all of our citizens.[3]

In a somewhat different sphere, we should also make certain that enough time, energy, and resources are being devoted to research programs dealing with technical aspects of disarmament and—highly important—that the personnel involved is sympathetic to the goals envisioned. Are we making an adequate effort, for example, in the study and development of verification procedures? Since we are striving for an agreement to prevent the spread of nuclear weapons, are we developing the means to make it effective? If we are to press persistently, as I hope we do, for a comprehensive test-ban treaty, are we moving fast enough in the necessary seismological research and in devising distant instrumentation? Are we being adventurous on a large enough scale in the further development of new scientific devices? Should we support the creation of more comprehensive verification

[3] *Report of the Committee on the Economic Impact of Defense and Disarmament* (Washington: July 1965), p. 8.

procedures by the IAEA to make sure that fissionable material is really being used for "peaceful purposes" and induce the U.S.S.R. the European Atomic Energy Community (Euratom), India, Israel, the U.A.R., and others to accept them, without exceptions? What about the development of "key diagnostic" inspection methods, or the transfer of inspection methods, such as surprise audits in banking and industrial inventory control by banking examiners or independent accountants, to the field of armaments and nuclear reactor control? What is "enough" can never be answered in any fixed or final way, being dependent on the priorities assigned to the elments of our disarmament policies.

It cannot be repeated often enough that we must constantly be reassessing our research projects and their support, to make as certain as possible that our policy priorities are accurately reflected in research priorities. One might add here that strong support for the Arms Control and Disarmament Agency is essential, as there is no other place in government where objective attention is continually focused first and foremost on disarmament.

Finally, we should never stop re-evaluating our disarmament proposals, both general and limited, in the light of advancing science and technology and of changing demands on our resources. The passage of time and the efforts of others might make certain weapons less important and others more so, as we are currently finding out in Viet-Nam and in space research. On the other hand, changing circumstances might increase responsibilities along certain lines. For example, we should keep a close scrutiny on the question of how many men under arms we may actually need and whether the maximum number which we have proposed for Stage I in our draft outline disarmament treaty would be sufficient to meet these world-wide responsibilities. If trouble spots continue to erupt, as they have in the Congo, Cyprus, Viet-Nam, the Dominican Republic, the Indian subcontinent, and Rhodesia, and there is no developed peace-keeping procedure in the United Nations or the Organization of American States, can we realistically expect to meet the demands on our armed forces?

Prospects for Limited Measures

As for our posture at the conference table, we should of course make it entirely clear to the whole world that we are eager to continue our discussion of both general disarmament and limited measures in the Eighteen-Nation Disarmament Committee in Geneva. It is to limited measures, however, that our main attention should be turned as offering a better promise of early agreement.

To be sure, the limited proposals of both the United States and the Soviet Union reflect the same conflicting aims evident in their long-term proposals and raise many of the same questions. But there are some common or parallel interests. Both powers seek to avoid major nuclear war and to reduce the terrible burden of the arms race. This is the situation which has produced the partial test ban and the pledge not to place nuclear weapons on vehicles orbiting in outer space. We have not had as much success in checking the spread of nuclear weapons, or with proposed steps to reduce the risk of war through accident, miscalculation, failure of communication, or surprise attack. During 1964, however, a more relaxed atmosphere made possible a series of actions—some taken unilaterally and others in concert with Moscow following diplomatic consultation—that seemed to be based on a new awareness that the two nations must learn to live together in peace in the same world.

On January 8, 1964, President Johnson announced a cutback in the production of enriched uranium by 25 per cent and the shutting down of four plutonium piles. Later in the same month, in a message to the reconvening Eighteen-Nation Disarmament Committee, the President placed strong emphasis on the exploration of a "verified freeze of the number and characteristics of strategic nuclear offensive and defensive vehicles," as well as on certain other points.

In early February the American representative at Geneva announced that the United States was willing to allow international inspection by the IAEA of one of the four nuclear reactors it was shutting down, whether the Soviet Union reciprocated or not, although it was freely admitted that the United States placed great importance on this step as a precedent and example. On March 5, 1964, the United States announced that it was opening to international inspection the large American nuclear reactor owned by the Yankee Atomic Electric Company at Rowe, Massachusetts, and urged the Soviet Union to reciprocate. This inspection has been carried out by the IAEA. So far, however, there has been no responsive action on the part of the Soviet Union.

In the meantime, a confidential correspondence had been going on between the White House and the Kremlin which resulted in the separate but synchronized announcement on April 20, 1964, of various measures of reduction in the production of fissionable materials by the United States and the Soviet Union, with the participation of Great Britain. These announcements did not deal with existing stockpiles, nor did they contain agreed arrangments on the question of inspection and verification.

It is probably correct to say that before 1963 it would not have been possible for such steps to have been taken. Encouraging as they may have seemed when taken, however, one should not forget that in this field steps taken by mutual example can be of only limited value if they are to continue to consist, on the Soviet side, of unverified statements, unsupported promises, and unpoliced statements of intent. On some subjects we may not need international verification or exact data, or we may be able to get what we need through national means. In such cases, depending on the particular circumstances, there may be value in being able to register the mere fact of being able to agree to similar steps on a reciprocal basis. But in many matters, especially where fundamental national safety, even survival, is involved, the policy of unverified mutual example can be said to have had only a very limited usefulness.

What of the future? Up to October 1964, when Khrushchev was deposed, one might have predicted that the time was ripening for additional agreements on limited measures of arms control or disarmament. It seemed as though both the United States and the Soviet Union had decided to proceed on the basis of a realization that, since general and complete disarmament was remote and the dangers to peace were immediate, it was wise to reduce those dangers at points where the common interest in doing so was apparent to both sides. In a different situation following the more recent events in Viet-Nam and elsewhere, it may be wise to wait until we can judge more clearly the temper of the leadership in the Soviet Union, the French challenge to NATO, the outcome of the crises in Viet-Nam and other points of conflict, and the effects of all these developments on the policies of Moscow and of Peking.

Nevertheless, some of the factors that seemed favorable to agreement in 1963 and 1964 still remain. There are signs that the economic aspects of arms reduction have come more and more under consideration in both Moscow and Washington. The Soviet government is contending with serious industrial and agricultural difficulties, to say nothing of problems of leadership in the Communist camp. On our side, President Johnson is placing heavy emphasis on his Great Society programs. The desirability of cutting the arms budget, if at all possible in view of the heavy commitment in Viet-Nam, has been apparent. It must be added, soberly but emphatically, that we should never succumb to the temptation to deal with fundamental military needs and arms levels, in relation to Communist purposes, primarily on the basis of domestic political considerations. Finally—and this is very important—the United States by 1965 had entered on a period in which it was clearly no longer necessary to keep the production of fissionable material at the level that had previously been considered essential to meet the requirements of our armed forces.

As we stand watchful and waiting for a clarification of the political trends, there are various limited measures which we can and should support without undue delay, though with different degrees of emphasis and with different estimates of the possibility of agreement. Generally speaking, we should press most strongly for those measures which are useful to us and which might seem to be easiest to negotiate with the Soviet Union. This statement should not be misconstrued to mean that only measures which meet both these criteria should be advocated. We cannot confine ourselves to measures which we think will be acceptable to the Soviet Union, both because to do so would assign to Soviet policies too great a determining role in our own and because we cannot give up the possibility, while maintaining our full military strength and capabilities, of persuading Soviet leaders to change their views with changing conditions.

For the reasons already cited, unless there should be a far-reaching reappraisal of national interest and national outlook on the part of Soviet leaders, there is very little hope for agreement on measures which would require considerable on-the-spot verification or elaborate inventories of armaments with full monitoring of the agreed inventory levels. In other words, no early agreement can be expected on proposals for a "freeze" in the production of offensive and defensive nuclear delivery vehicles, as put forward in the United States draft outline of April 1962, for an immediate 30 per cent reduction in nuclear delivery vehicles, for a cutback in the production of fissionable material, for a reduction of atomic materials with verification by inspection, or for a reduction in the production of uranium and plutonium. Proposals for inspection through budgetary examination also do not seem promising, in view of the quite short and inexplicit Soviet military budget and their placing of what we would call military items in scientific programs not within the purview of agreement.

Some Concrete Suggestions

There are, however, a number of limited measures on which there may be a stronger ray of hope. A comprehensive test-ban treaty is one. Others have been touched on in Chapter III. Still others should be noted here.

1. *Destruction of certain existing weapons.* This is an approach that may prove useful in the future. It should be noted, however, that time has erased the value of a reciprocal "bomber bonfire" of an equal number of B-47 and TU-16 bombers, as proposed by the United States in March 1964. Obsolescence has accomplished what could not be agreed on. As the late Adlai Stevenson reported to the Disarmament Commission on April 26, 1965, by mid-1966 the United States will have inactivated or destroyed more than two thousand B-47 bomber-type aircraft and will also

have reduced the number of B-52 heavy-bomber aircraft. However, as he also pointed out, there is a limit to unilateral restraints;[4] and new situations, such as the conflict in Viet-Nam, are requiring us to replace existing aircraft with more modern types. It is not clear what action, if any, the Soviet Union has been taking in regard to destroying certain existing weapons.

2. *Production controls.* As has already been pointed out above, the United States has shut down certain production facilities for fissionable material and opened some to international inspection. The Soviet Union has also announced the shutdown of certain similar facilities but has not offered to open them to verification and international inspection.

It may prove to be not impossible to negotiate some inspection of the closed-down facilities, perhaps for specific and limited purposes and at specific locations, to which access could be controlled by the host nation. There may be some merit in pressing for reciprocal, instead of international, inspection of closed-down plants. A procedure in which each side inspects the other is simpler in many ways and would result in direct and immediate reports to each national government by persons whom it had itself chosen.

3. *A verified freeze on the number and characteristics of strategic nuclear delivery vehicles.* As has been pointed out a number of times, this seems the place to begin, for such vehicles represent the greatest destructive force. The United States has already submitted a great deal of information on how such "an agreement could be adequately verified with a minimum amount of intrusion."[5]

4. *The transfer of fissionable materials to peaceful uses.* This is a field in which we should continue to make strong efforts, as we have in the past. Now that the production of fissionable material has exceeded immediate weapons needs, it would seem an especially propitious time to press ahead. In an effort to meet Soviet objections, Ambassador Arthur J. Goldberg stated before a

[4] Speech of April 26, 1965, DC/PV. 73, Verbatim Record of 73rd Meeting, p. 25.

[5] Same, p. 21. Information was submitted at the 211th Meeting of the ENDC on August 21, 1964.

plenary session of the UN General Assembly on September 23, 1965, that "the United States is ready to transfer 60,000 kilograms of weapons-grade U-235 to nonweapon uses if the Soviet Union would be willing to transfer 40,000 kilograms." We should seek to have this material transferred to the IAEA or placed under an effective system of IAEA safeguards. A month later the United States expanded its proposal when William C. Foster suggested in the First Committee that "the fissionable material to be transferred to peaceful uses be removed from actual weapons and that the weapons themselves—the casings and internal mechanism—be destroyed." The destruction of "several thousand weapons" by each side would be carried out in the presence of observers from the other "in such a way that secret design features of the weapons are not revealed."[6]

However valuable such a step would be, it should be pointed out that it is not likely to be acceptable to the Soviet Union as long as we do not make public in general terms how much fissionable material we actually have, how much we believe the other side to have and, therefore, how much of a difference such a reduction would actually make to us and to them, and what effect it would have on relative Soviet strength in this field. Thus far the transfer idea has not scored much of a success either with the Soviet Union or with other nations, who can see this aspect of superior U.S. stockpiles perfectly clearly. The experience reinforces my own skepticism with respect to proposals made for "public relations" purposes rather than on a realistic, objective, long-term basis. Disarmament negotiations should not be a poker game in which you "call" your adversary. To succeed, each step must be soberly and carefully verified.

5. *Measures for the reduction of the risk of war through accidents, miscalculation, failure of communication, and surprise attack.* This is a subject in which the United States has long maintained an interest and has advanced a number of proposals going back to the 1950s. Although the Soviet Union has on occasion expressed some approval of the idea of observation posts and the exchange of military missions, agreement has so far proved impossible. And yet, in this day of "instantaneous mili-

---

[6] *Department of State Bulletin,* October 11, 1965, pp. 583-584; *The New York Times,* October 28, 1965.

tary response," it would seem in the interest of both sides to reduce the possibility of misinterpretation of what might be an innocent action, an accident, or a miscalculation; and to provide additional time wherever possible for the true evaluation of all events. Much can be done in this regard by unilateral measures, but international agreement can also play a significant role in preventing suspicion, draining it off where it is unwarranted, and providing correct advance information of a reassuring nature concerning certain events such as military or naval maneuvers.

Both the American and Soviet drafts on general disarmament contain provisions covering these questions, each from the point of view of its own security arrangements and its own ultimate aims. Thus the United States draft provides that the parties would "give advance notification of major military movements and maneuvers" to other parties and to the proposed International Disarmament Organization. A closely related measure would provide for the establishment of observation posts, to be set up at agreed locations, "including major ports, railway centers, motor highways, river crossings, and air bases to report on concentrations and movements of military forces."

The Soviet draft has a somewhat different slant. It contains a flat prohibition "from the commencement of the first stage" of "large-scale joint military movements or maneuvers by armed forces of two or more States," a provision which, if adopted, would largely do away with the military aspects of NATO but would not apply to movements or maneuvers by a single state with vast territory such as the U.S.S.R. The Soviet draft also proposes that parties to the treaty agree to "give advance notification of large-scale military movements or maneuvers by their national armed forces within their national frontiers." There are also suggestions for the exchange of military missions by both sides.

There is good reason to press hard toward agreement on some aspect of this subject. It is worthwhile in itself, it should contribute to the security of both sides, and the occasional expressions of interest by Premier Khrushchev at least opened up the possibility that the Soviet government might slowly be coming to the point of serious negotiation.

It should be emphasized, however, that it would be better to have no agreement at all than one which would result in unsatisfactory performance and a false sense of security on the part of the West. For example, if there are to be observation posts, the observers must have sufficient freedom of movement, of communication, and of access to make their presence really meaningful. If the observers are to be, so to speak, "confined to barracks," without "eyes," we would be better off not having them at all. We must avoid at all costs so-called "face-saving" or "public relations" agreements, which are in fact self-deceiving.

6. *Exchange of information on military budgets.* This practice could be helpful *provided* the Soviet budget were as open to us as ours is to them. This would probably be considered "intrusive" by Soviet authorities and therefore unacceptable.

7. *Exchange of scientific and other information.* We should press for an exchange of information between the United States and the Soviet Union on a variety of topics of mutual interest or of potential mutual interest. This exchange should take place in a quiet, nonpolemic fashion, preferably between small groups of specialists. Perhaps there might be in some cases joint research groups which might at least acquaint each other with their respective points of view and become acquainted on a personal basis. As was stated in the earlier chapter on negotiation, there is something to be gained by making Soviet leaders feel more at home with representatives of what they call the "capitalist world." This might be one way of doing it, though it is obviously impossible to guarantee any results. It is clear that there would be no value to such exchanges if they were allowed to degenerate into a mere repetition of political slogans.

8. *The nondissemination of nuclear weapons to non-nuclear states.* Although when taken separately each of the various measures suggested for this purpose is of a limited character, the entire "package" assumes such large proportions that this supremely important topic of nondissemination is reserved for the concluding chapter.

*   *   *

In working on limited measures, we would also be trying to make some headway toward the distant goal of disarmament in a peaceful world. That will mean more marathon negotiations, for which, unfortunately, there can be no guarantee of success. We can only keep on trying to the best of our abilities and energy. There is risk in this effort, certainly, whether we make progress or whether we do not. But are the alternatives any less risky or more promising?

Chapter VII

The Urgent Future

Past policies or steps which flow directly from those policies have been our concern in the preceding chapters. In many aspects of disarmament and arms control the United States has offered carefully thought-out programs; their only fault is that they have not been adopted. At the same time it is clear that we cannot afford to stand still. If we are to deal with the arms problems of an era which promises to be even less manageable and more clamorous than the recent past, we must make a new kind of effort, rethink major aspects of our foreign policy, and engage in a sustained diplomatic campaign to advance our goals.

In the arms field there is one problem which overrides all others in urgency: preventing the further proliferation of nuclear weapons. We are now face to face with a prospect which President Kennedy called "the greatest possible danger and hazard" —a time when the number of nations both willing and able to acquire stocks of nuclear weapons may increase substantially. If we are to prevent further proliferation, we must move quickly and drastically, or run the grave risk that in a few years the situation will be permanently out of hand. Some say that it is already too late. We must make the most strenuous endeavors to prove them wrong. The submission of a brief draft treaty at Geneva on August 17, 1965, is a sign that the United States government is cognizant of the problem. We must not allow our efforts on nonproliferation to flag merely because of the summary rejection of that draft by the Soviet Union or because of our problem with West Germany's aspirations for a greater share or "appropriate part" in NATO nuclear strategy.

Article I of the proposed treaty on the nonproliferation of nuclear weapons provides:

> Each of the nuclear states party to this treaty undertakes not to transfer any nuclear weapons into the national control of any non-nuclear state, either directly or indirectly through a military alliance; and each undertakes not to take any other action which would cause an increase in the total number of states and other organizations having independent power to use nuclear weapons.

The important words are "national control" and "increase." Thus, if there were to be a veto-free nuclear force within NATO, the United States, Britain, or France would, under the proposed treaty, have to surrender the "independent power to use nuclear weapons." There would appear to be little likelihood that the Congress would approve the surrender of national control over U.S. nuclear weapons, and General de Gaulle appears adamant about retaining and increasing France's nuclear power. That would leave Great Britain holding the key to whether a veto-free NATO nuclear force might ever evolve, because NATO as an organization would in effect replace Britain as the world's fifth nuclear power if there is to be no "increase in the total number of states and other organizations having independent power to use nuclear weapons."

Great Britain did not agree to co-sponsor our draft treaty to prevent the spread of nuclear weapons. Lord Chalfont, the British delegate, said in Geneva that it "does not rule out the possibility that an association of states could by a majority decision use nuclear weapons." Washington, which has not itself proposed a European or veto-free NATO nuclear force but does not wish to foreclose for all time that possibility, believes that it is now only theoretical. But Lord Chalfont said Britain prefers that "this door be closed."

There is continuing popular feeling in Britain, almost as strong as in the Soviet Union, against the Germans getting a "finger on the nuclear trigger," and Britain would like to have an explicit provision that any multilateral nuclear group in NATO would be governed by a British and American veto on the use of nuclear weapons, which obviously would not satisfy West Germany as a permanent arrangement. The Soviet position is that there must be no transfer, direct or indirect, of nuclear weapons to third states or groups of states including alliances. The Soviet Union, of course, is out to prevent any NATO nuclear force, no matter what the voting safeguards on its use may be. Nor does it put faith in Germany's legal obligation to other Western powers not to manufacture atomic weapons.

Washington has apparently not as yet decided that the time is right for a supreme and unconditional effort to win an antiproliferation agreement. Unfortunately, by the time the text of a treaty is threshed out to meet the ideas of Great Britain, France, West Germany, and the U.S.S.R., especially in view of the general resistance to accepting international controls, nuclear proliferation among nations may be far more widespread than it is now.

The question is so important that we ought to use our best efforts to bring about the desired result. Delay may make the problem almost insoluble. As President Johnson said in his message proposing the draft of August 17, 1965, "The peace of the world requires firm limits upon the spread of nuclear weapons. . . . The time is now. The hour is late. The fate of generations yet unborn is in our hands."

This is more than a matter of willingness to negotiate. If there is any lesson in the preceding chapters, it is that fundamental progress in disarmament and arms control will not be achieved at the negotiating table alone. Specific proposals will be honed, polished, and prepared for agreement there, and that is a necessary and important process. But the decision to agree, or indeed to continue the talks at all, will depend on other things. Thus, if we want to prevent the proliferation of nuclear weapons or indeed to get action on any other aspects of arms problems, it is primarily to the basic political relations of nations, East and West, that we must look rather than to the discussions at Geneva. In practical terms, it is the totality of our relations with the Soviet Union and the Communist world and with our allies that is here involved.

In these relations we stand again at a moment of great uncertainty. We do not know whether the Soviet Union will elect to turn more toward the West or toward the East, or what will be the real content of its proclaimed policy of peaceful coexistence as time goes on. The Soviet Union is, as George F. Kennan put it, "enmeshed in a veritable welter of contradictions and problems" which may make its behavior "in part the product of the way we ourselves play our hand and in this sense susceptible in some degree to our influence."[1] It is our duty, to ourselves and to the future, to probe for every opportunity to exercise such influence and to seek out areas of agreement if they exist. It is our duty, in other words, to look at the entire pattern of our relations with the Soviet Union to see, without any illusions, whether and in what ways we can draw that vast country closer to the West to forestall any movement toward collision with us.

The Dangers and the Remedy

Let us take these two problems—nonproliferation of nuclear weapons and our relations with the Soviet Union—in tandem, starting with the former.

We are accustomed to thinking of nations which do not produce nuclear weapons as "non-nuclear." This is an error. Although nuclear weapons production may for the moment be limited to a few nations, the latter through their "atoms for peace" programs, their joint nuclear power and desalinization programs, and their sale of fissionable materials have allowed others to develop a nuclear capacity also. These states are nuclear states. Since the atom is "neutral," since the basic know-how of weapons production is generally available, and since the production of weapons-grade plutonium is steadily becoming both easier and cheaper, it follows that a number of so-called "non-nuclear" states have the capacity now to move into nuclear weapons production, should they decide it is in their interest to do so.

Although there are various reasons weighing against such a decision, not one state has acted in such a way as to foreclose its option; and some, despite public statements to the contrary, are taking more positive steps. Under present conditions there is no

---

[1] Walter E. Edge Lecture, "The United States and the Communist Giants," Princeton University, February 25, 1965 (unpublished).

institutionalized way of stopping them, since existing systems of safeguards, bilateral or international, are still very primitive or problematical.

For a responsible power such as the United States, interested both in keeping the peace and in maintaining an environment in which it is possible to live in freedom, there is much to ponder in this prospect. The peace of the world is precarious enough at present, with nuclear weapons in the hands of five powers. Could there be anything but even greater danger if such weapons were in the possession of a host of smaller states intent on the pursuit of their local or regional aims and possibly unrestrained by the sober considerations which have so far prevailed, despite some dangerous moments, in the nuclear relations of the United States, the United Kingdom, and the Soviet Union? To realize how close to the edge of chaos we would all be living, one has only to imagine President Sukarno brandishing nuclear threats at Malaysia, or Israel and the Arab states adding nuclear as well as economic blackmail to their arsenals, or Communist China or some other state bent on power smuggling nuclear arms into an internecine African struggle. To say this is not to imply a false optimism about relations among the larger powers or a lessened concern about other weapons or the need for their control. Obviously not. It is merely to point out how urgent it is to prevent the further spread of nuclear weapons while the possibility of doing so still exists.

This possibility will be translated into reality only if there is a willingness to pay the costs of Draconian and unprecedented measures bound to impinge on the freedom of action of our own and of other nations. The broad obligations contained in the American draft treaty submitted at Geneva would have to be supplemented by detailed arrangements. Perhaps it would require a world-wide cutting off of all international transfers of ownership or possession of nuclear weapons and fissionable material, and all trade in some types of machinery, computers, dual-purpose nuclear reactors, and raw materials useful in the manufacture of nuclear weapons; a prohibition on any assistance by mathematicians, computer experts, scientists, or technical personnel which could be useful in helping a country move toward nuclear weapons production; and a world-wide ban on all test explosions for weapons.

Although some steps could be taken by the United States alone, logically and practically there would have to be international agreement with the participation of all weapons-producing states, as well as of countries with important deposits of raw materials or stocks of fissionable materials or with the capability of producing them. Other states would be invited to join in the agreement, but, if need be, the nuclear states would have to take the ultimate responsibility of enforcing it.

To buttress whatever procedures might be worked out, there would have to be intensive, objective, and expert inspection of the nuclear production facilities of countries or atomic agencies not producing nuclear weapons. Such a proposal might well arouse the strongest protests from some (especially from Euratom, Israel, or India) and charges of "atomic monopoly," but surely there is a larger goal here that is in the common interest of all peoples. We must do all we can to convince every nation of the priority of the pre-eminent requirements of world peace.

All can share in the working out of fair and effective procedures of inspection and enforcement. We have still a great deal of work to do in this field. We should look carefully into the techniques by which bank examiners "blanket" a bank for a period of one or two weeks, in effect taking auditing control over its operations in their entirety and checking or test-checking as necessary every aspect of activity. We should push for regular reports from the facilities, at whatever intervals are necessary, and for surprise visits by inspectors with complete auditing or inspection powers. We should bend every effort toward strengthening the inspection powers of the IAEA, so that it may come to exercise a real, even if limited, police power. Effective controls would have to be established over the facilities of Euratom, as well as over all other relevant agencies. The Soviet refusal to recognize Euratom's existence is a roadblock to effective international inspection procedures which we should attempt to clear away.

Generally speaking, we should try in every way possible to ensure that so-called nonmilitary nuclear production is not allowed to continue under the insufficient procedures of inspection which have hitherto prevailed. This is not to say that the international "atoms for peace" program would have to come to an end. If it can be restricted by adopting greater frequency of inspection by competent and objective observers in order to prevent the diversion of fissionable materials from peaceful to military uses, and with a prompt triggering of IAEA sanctions if such diversion is found, then it should be pushed. The real question is, can it be so restricted? IAEA or other inspection would have to be more frequent, with the IAEA system expanded and perfected to encompass new types of facilities, particularly large fabrication and reprocessing plants, and possibly with the development of better instruments to reduce the need for trained manpower.

Atom-Free Zones

Another constructive step would be the establishment of atom-free zones in Latin America and Africa, though we should recognize that such zones would be meaningless and might even be dangerous unless there were effective inspection and unless all the countries in the regions involved were willing to participate honestly in the agreement. Europe is a different problem. The various versions of the Rapacki Plan, whether for a "denuclearization" or for a "freeze" (the so-called Gomulka Plan), are too one-sided for our serious consideration.[2] Their clear aim is to emasculate NATO's nuclear strength while leaving undisturbed the hundreds of solid-fuel MRBMs or Polaris-type missiles presently aimed at Western Europe from Soviet territory.

The original Rapacki proposals provided for a total ban on nuclear weapons in a Central European zone including West and East Germany, plus Poland and Czechoslovakia. Given the vast hinterland stretching behind Eastern Europe, compared with the narrow hinterland behind West Germany (to the Atlantic), the

[2] For the Rapacki Plan texts, see Department of State, *Documents on Disarmament, 1945-1959*, v. II (Washington: GPO, 1960), pp. 889-892, 944-948, and 1217-1219; for the Gomulka Plan, see Embassy of the Polish People's Republic, Washington, Press Release, March 6, 1964.

meaning of this proposal is in effect to place the Federal Republic and NATO at a great military disadvantage. It means also, given the present negative attitude of the French government toward non-French nuclear weapons on French territory, the effective nuclear disarmament of NATO forces on the European continent, for the only change on the other side would be the removal of any Soviet missiles with nuclear warheads from East Germany, Poland, and Czechoslovakia.

The proposal for a "freeze" in a similar zone, while superficially more attractive in permitting retention of existing weapons and one-for-one replacement for maintenance, is in reality merely a variation on the same basic theme of undercutting NATO's nuclear power. In such circumstances NATO's nuclear strength would deteriorate, while there would be no restraints on nuclear armaments inside the U.S.S.R., where such arms are constantly improving. One can only conclude that unless and until proposals for the creation of a "denuclearized" zone in Europe include the western parts of the Soviet Union, they will not merit serious consideration on the part of the United States or its allies.

A comprehensive nuclear test-ban treaty to bind all nations, which has already been suggested as a desirable goal of further negotiations with the Soviet Union, would also be a major step toward preventing the spread of nuclear weapons.

Persuasion and Guarantees

Let us also consider the matter from the standpoint of the states for which the possibility of going into nuclear weapons production is a real one. History is bare of examples in which nations have formally agreed ahead of time to give up the entire possibility of developing or acquiring a particular type of weapon, except as the result of military defeat and thus only under duress. That they are still reluctant to do so was made very clear in the discussion in 1961 of the Swedish proposal for a "non-nuclear club." The gradual "shrinkage" over the years of the resolutions on this subject put forward in the General Assembly also bears witness to the lack of enthusiasm for the idea of giving up the possibility of nuclear weapons in return for the creation of "areas of law" protected by great-power guarantee. The difficult problem before us is to maintain or create conditions in which states without nuclear weapons will neither want to acquire them nor be able to do so.

Furthermore, if we are really concerned with trying to do everything in our power to prevent the further spread of these weapons, the U.S. government may have to make it clear after careful study of pertinent treaties and international law, publicly or confidentially as circumstances require, that in the event of a nuclear attack on a non-nuclear state this country itself would be prepared to take necessary steps, possibly including a counter-strike against the attacker. This may be the only way to cope with the use of nuclear blackmail, which it does not take clairvoyance to anticipate from Communist China or Indonesia or in the Middle East.

President Johnson put it this way: "The nations that do not seek national nuclear weapons can be sure that, if they need our strong support against some threat of nuclear blackmail, then they will have it."[3]

As can readily be seen, for both the United States and for nations without nuclear weapons the problem of preventing further proliferation poses remarkable, unprecedented problems and responsibilities.

Although the United States could set some of these recommendations in motion by itself, it is apparent that the participation of a number of other nations is necessary if real success is to be achieved in this path-breaking task. Perhaps France will gradually come to a reconsideration of its position. The problem of the participation of Communist China poses a different set of difficulties. Clearly, the possibilities of nuclear threats or attacks against its neighbors, or the use of Chinese nuclear weapons in an area of greater radius, are matters of utmost relevance. Logically, no system for the nonproliferation of nuclear weapons can succeed over the long run without the participation of Peking. But we should not refrain, because of the totally negative atti-

[3] Address by the President, October 18, 1964, in *Department of State Bulletin*, November 2, 1964, p. 613.

tude of Peking, from moving forward in the quest for agreement with the Soviet Union. Perhaps it is only when some success is obtained in that direction that the problem of China will become a manageable one.

Even though Communist China can as yet possess only a tiny nuclear arsenal, the bomb which was exploded in October 1964 was more than a primitive atomic device, and the one dropped in May 1965 was detonated from an airplane. Secretary of Defense McNamara, in a statement to NATO in December 1965, said that the Chinese could start a small stockpile of atomic weapons and develop operational medium-range ballistic missiles within the next two years.[4] Furthermore, it should not be forgotten that, depending on one's targets and purpose, a highly developed delivery system is not a *sine qua non* for the use of atomic bombs against an enemy. If the target is close enough and if there is no developed defensive air force, an atomic bomb could be delivered by any plane large enough to carry it, with minor alterations. Nor should we overlook the possibility of nuclear attack on a "one-shot" basis through the use of a submarine launching a missile from the ocean's surface. Although Communist China will probably not have any real or sustained capacity to make nuclear missiles for submarines for some time, it is always possible that it might be able to make a few for tactical purposes. Against such threats, the informal guarantee mentioned above could serve a purpose. In the absence of agreements, we shall have to cope with such situations as best we can. But we should not lose sight of the ultimate goal of bringing China, with the Soviet Union and with potential nuclear powers, into an effective international system.

The problem of the security of Southeast Asia and indeed of Asia as a whole is, of course, much more than a matter of inhibiting nuclear attack by Communist China. There are, as we all know, countless other methods of aggression and subversion. It may well be that Chinese Communist pressure on Southeast Asia, where China exercised a vague suzerainty before the British and French colonial era, will continue no matter what our policy toward Peking or toward Viet-Nam. Marshall Chen Yi, Commu-

[4] *The New York Times,* December 16, 1965.

nist China's Foreign Minister, has already announced that Thailand is to be the next target for "liberation," and Communist activity there has increased.

In view of the important doctrinal statement by Marshal Lin Piao, the Chinese Communist Defense Minister, that Peking's support of revolutionary wars in undeveloped countries is a strategy directed at the eventual encirclement of the United States and Western Europe in accordance with Mao Tse-tung's well-known Marxist-Leninist theories, and that the imperialists "will be swept like dust from the stage of history by the mighty broom of the revolutionary people,"[5] it is apparent that the Chinese Communists are using the situation in Viet-Nam in a conscious endeavor to prove that so-called wars of "national liberation" can be won against "imperialist nuclear powers."

Certainly, attempts at more friendly relations by Western nations which have recognized Peking have not been notably successful. Nor is it true that "we cannot talk" with the Chinese because we have not recognized them. We did so at Panmunjom, at Geneva in 1954, and our Ambassador in Warsaw continues the long-standing series of talks with the Communist Chinese Ambassador to Poland. Whatever we do, Communist China seems bent on continuing its hostile and revolutionary course. Nor is it a country, in view of the record, to which the American people can look with much confidence. Its diplomatic recognition by the United States and admission into the United Nations would meet with the disapproval of a large number of Americans. Even discussion of this matter raises the hackles of many prominent citizens. However, if only because the problem of bringing a viable peace to Southeast Asia must be solved, we should not fall into the trap of considering our policy toward Communist China as frozen, as having reached a kind of eternal balance between advantage and disadvantage. We should always be acutely alert to any changes that might take place in Communist China among the leadership groups, in ideology or in policy.

[5] Published in *Hung Chi*, the ideological journal of the Central Committee of the Chinese Communist party, and in all major Chinese newspapers on September 3, 1965; English translation in *Peking Review*, September 3, 1965, pp. 9-30.

Our own national sovereignty has never been challenged. As a people we tend to believe we can maintain a lofty policy of principle, unrelated to power and changing conditions. It is doubtful that we can remain so aloof. Our very existence may be threatened. To survive, we must retain a watchful awareness of developments so as not to be blinded to our own disadvantage by conceptions which may lose their value with the passage of time. In other words, like every aspect of our foreign policy, our policy toward Communist China, and toward our ally, the Chinese government on Taiwan, to which we owe much, must remain under a continuing and watchful appraisal.[6]

The Political Issues in Europe

Now let us turn to the question of relations with the Soviet Union in the context of the present discussion. Although there are some steps that the United States might take without the cooperation of the Soviet government, it cannot deal with non-proliferation in Europe or with any of the more far-reaching means to curb such proliferation anywhere in the world without having to consider Soviet foreign policy and the aims and fears of those who make it. Indeed, it may be impossible to make progress toward our own goals without reconsidering and continually testing our policy toward the Soviet Union and keeping open possibilities that may have more hopeful prospects than those we can see at present.

The core of the problem of a political *détente* or settlement with Russia, like that of preventing the spread of nuclear weapons, lies in Europe and the reunification of Germany. On the one side is the United States, which stands clearly against the further proliferation of nuclear weapons but has also sponsored for a long time a NATO multilateral nuclear force (MLF), in which West Germany would be a major partner though not itself having control of nuclear weapons. On the other side is the Soviet Union, which also says it is in favor of preventing further

[6] For a decade I have held this general view on Communist China and the protection of Nationalist China. See my article, "United States Foreign Policy and Formosa," *Foreign Affairs*, April 1955, pp. 360-375.

proliferation but opposes MLF, inside or outside NATO, as in reality meaning just that further proliferation. As long as the United States continues support for MLF, or for some equivalent to it if MLF itself is dropped, the Soviet position is that it will not consider any nonproliferation agreement with the United States.

Bearing in mind that it is in the Soviet interest to wreck, if possible, any scheme intended to strengthen the NATO alliance or the West generally, we have to consider objectively whether the MLF, or something like it, is really as vital to Western security, to the future of NATO, and to the satisfaction of West Germany as its sponsors claim. There is no wisdom in giving Moscow a veto on how the West organizes for its own defense. It is wise, however, to weigh Soviet reactions and to see what advantages there may be for us in alternative courses of action, especially if we believe in the prime importance of preventing the further proliferation of nuclear weapons.

No matter how one puts it, it seems to me that there is a deep contradiction between our professions on the extreme importance of the nonproliferation of nuclear weapons and our proposals for further nuclear sharing in NATO, as discussed earlier in this chapter. The motives for MLF were excellent: to meet the desire of our European allies for a greater participation in the strategic nuclear affairs of the alliance and to quiet some of their fears as to the reliability of our nuclear support, to keep West Germany an active, satisfied member of NATO, and to give support to moderate political elements in that country. The Soviet Union's real interests, also, would be better served by such a West Germany than by one disassociated from the West and playing a lone-wolf role, seeking its advantage in the blackmailing of either East or West or both.

We should not cease to remind the Soviet leaders of that basic truth, however unwilling they seem to be to recognize it. In any case, events have shown that in MLF we had a policy which gave us the worst of both worlds. Except in West Germany, it has attracted very little support among our allies and also a good deal of protest from the Soviet Union, which is not, I believe, merely for the record. The Soviet fear of a nuclear-armed Germany is deep-rooted and not to be ignored in its effects on all other aspects of Soviet-Western relations. The British are more polite, but their fears of a united, nuclear-armed Germany are also deep-seated.

So we come here to a question of priorities and of emphasis. In effect, we have to decide which is more important: pursuit of an agreement on nonproliferation with the Soviet Union (and others) or a policy under which West Germany gains an ever stronger position within the Western alliance and comes closer to having nuclear weapons of its own, to the accompaniment of both Soviet disquiet and uneasiness among our allies. If we decide that preventing the spread of nuclear weapons is the most urgent goal, we should look for other effective ways to organize Western defense and still achieve the political purposes that lay behind the MLF proposals. We cannot, of course, afford to push West Germany into a position of primary reliance on an independent policy rather than on NATO by a seeming neglect of German interests in our pursuit of a nonproliferation agreement with the Soviet Union. There is always the danger that neither major objective will be achieved, for the Soviets could in the end reject a nonproliferation agreement after we had risked a rupture of NATO solidarity in order to get it.

Secretary McNamara's suggestion at the end of May 1965 for a "Select Committee" in NATO on nuclear matters may prove at least a partial answer to the problem, especially if it can have a significant role in coordinating and planning policy on the use of nuclear weapons. The German Federal Republic must continue to be securely anchored in the Western alliance. Both Soviet and German leaders should be left in no doubt as to the firm American view on that score. At the same time we should at least try to convince the Soviet leaders, on the basis of historical evidence, that this is to their advantage as well as ours, and to show awareness of their concern.

Meanwhile, the United States should continue trying to help Western Europe toward a greater degree of unity, and to do what it can to bring about a free and united Germany, as part of an eventual Central European settlement. Only if there is a unified Germany, with a freely elected government, will it be possible to proceed to the signing of a peace treaty and the final settlement of the question of the German-Polish border.

Germany reunification, of course, raises the question of the relation of a unified Germany to NATO. As the Western powers have insisted in the past, Germany must have freedom to make its own choice. It is important to remember, however, that NATO was established as a means to an end and not as an end in itself. While the effort to achieve German unity is going on, we should also sit down, first by ourselves and then with our NATO allies, to review the entire NATO structure and the commitments of each member elsewhere, in the light of the needs which have developed over the years and which are not now being met by the alliance or by individual policies, and taking account of the changes occurring in the Communist world.

To mention only one relevant problem, it is obvious that the European concerns which led to our MLF proposal are still very much in evidence. It is not in the least surprising that the Western European nations are reluctant to accede to our request that, despite the Soviet threat, they agree not to have nuclear weapons while at the same time we refuse to give them a "finger on the trigger" or to spell out more precisely when the President of the United States will authorize use of the weapons.

Our problem is to work out a scheme by which the Western European nations will have a greater say in the use of nuclear weapons in their defense while the United States retains the weapons themselves in its own hands. We should therefore be giving serious consideration to the possibility of working out some such arrangement at a series of carefully prepared "summit" meetings of NATO, which would decide, for example, on certain "agreed events" in which the President of the United States would be empowered and instructed, ahead of time, to react with nuclear weapons.

This is just one possibility which we should be considering and discussing with our allies. It would require some difficult adjustments on all sides. There might be criticism in this country that it would extend our obligations too much and cut down on our freedom to act in certain crucial instances. But if NATO is to be effective and West Europeans are not to be regarded as puppets, we must face the problems of our day and show imagination and realism in trying to deal with them. If we are really interested in preventing the further proliferation of nuclear weapons, we must take full account of our allies' interest in a greater degree of control over nuclear weapons to be used in their defense. As a leader of the German Social Democratic Party has recently written, "The Multilateral Nuclear Force was a second-best alternative to the simpler solution of giving every partner in NATO— provided he is making a fair contribution to the conventional field—a say in the nuclear part of the strategy too." Ultimate decisions on the use of nuclear weapons would rest with the President of the United States, "acting as trustee for the alliance but basing his decision on a commonly agreed strategy."[7]

Existing organs and existing ways of acting are not sufficient to meet this challenge. In the absence of Western European political unity, we must seek to improvise adequate institutions as best we can. It is easy to criticize NATO but difficult to revitalize it. Let us give our best efforts and thoughts to the hard task. Let us move our attention from the daily details to the outlines of the structure as a whole.

American and Soviet Interests

To return again to the problem of our relations with the Soviet Union, let us start with a caveat. In the minds of certain people today, to think in a constructive way is "subversive." To be "anti" is enough. But to quiet the fears of those for whom any suggestion of closer relations or negotiated settlements with the Soviet Union raises only the most lurid possibilities, let me state quite clearly that no "appeasement" is contemplated, no slurring over the goals of the Soviet Union and of the world Communist movement that are basically hostile to us, and no lowering of our defensive capacities. In other words, this is no suggestion of a relationship based on a naïve faith in "peaceful coexistence" that overlooks its corollary, as Premier Khrushchev made clear in his speech of January 6, 1961, of "wars of national liberation," but

[7] Fritz Erler, "The Alliance and the Future of Germany," *Foreign Affairs*, April 1965, pp. 442-443.

a relationship based on a belief that communism cannot be defeated by military means alone and on rational, hardheaded calculation of national interests on both sides.

Just what are these national interests? For the Soviet Union they may well prove to be the raising of the standard of living at home, the avoidance of major war, the stalemating of Communist China, prevention of the rise of a powerful and hostile Germany, support for "national liberation" struggles (on an increasingly selective scale), and the maintenance of leadership in the world Communist movement against the challenge of the Chinese Communists.

For the United States they are to bring the Soviet Union to a less hostile and less dangerous policy toward the West, to avoid major war, to reach a more stable situation both in Europe and in Asia, to curb Communist China's expansionism, to keep the two major Communist powers at odds with each other rather than united against the West, to prevent the expansion of Communist power through the medium of "national liberation" struggles sponsored and supported from outside, and to create a more peaceful world atmosphere, in part through the prevention of further proliferation of nuclear weapons. Except on the question of the support for so-called wars of national liberation, there would seem to be sufficient common interest at least for some degree of cooperation.

If it is truly in our interest to bring the Soviet Union closer to the West as well as to try to prevent the further spread of nuclear weapons, should we not try to come to the recognition on both sides that there is no reasonable possibility of seeing the other disappear and that, without ignoring the differences in ideology or forgetting the realities of the cold war, there is an interest in making the world somewhat safer for both? The Soviets would have to put limits on their support of "national liberation" movements and other instruments of subversion, and we would devote ourselves to exploring all reasonable avenues of agreement.

Now it may be that the Soviet Union, even should it see some benefits in doing so, will not feel able to stop support for "wars of liberation" because of the challenge to its leadership among

Communists that has been mounted by Communist China. But this is something that we should find out not only through news reports and public statements but also through top-level talks between our leaders and those of the Soviet Union. As has already been pointed out, such talks should not take place until we can be sure that the present Soviet leadership is willing to proceed and until after we have conducted preliminary discussions within our own government, including leaders of the Congress, and with our allies.

If we should find preliminary talks with Moscow encouraging, we could then go on to more specific issues, such as stopping the spread of nuclear weapons, European security, a comprehensive test ban, and lesser matters that have led to suspicion and recrimination.

In addition, it may be in our interest to adopt a policy of increased trade in nonstrategic items with the Soviet Union, provided that country settles its Lend-Lease obligations and shows by its behavior that it is willing to carry out its obligations under whatever mutually satisfactory arrangements might prove possible. Our interest in trade with the Soviet Union would also be affected by Soviet policies on the other matters, such as payment of United Nations dues and policies toward United Nations peace-keeping forces, Berlin and the future of Germany, Cuba, and subversion in Latin America. Let us remember further that trading contacts are always more than just business contacts. They mean exposure to Western ideas and may increase our chances of exercising some influence on various aspects of Soviet life that may ultimately affect Soviet foreign policy.

There is thus a great web of complex and interrelated political issues to which the arts of diplomacy should be applied. To make any substantial progress on them, if it proves possible at all, will take much time. Yet the one burning question of nonproliferation of nuclear weapons cannot wait for years. Everything possible should be done to see what can be done about it now. But a favorable atmosphere for it depends so much on the general climate of Soviet-American relations and Soviet-Chinese relations that we should attempt to move forward on more than one front.

There are no circumstances in which it would be easy to pursue a course such as outlined above. At best, the Soviet Union is a skittish, difficult, and basically hostile adversary, accustomed to regarding the West with extreme suspicion and skepticism. Even with an aggressive China at its back and a strong need for trade with the West, the Soviet Union may be expected to move slowly, perhaps even stop formal disarmament discussions entirely for a while. If this happens, we should seek to move the talks to other channels of negotiation. We must continue to make a strenuous and imaginative effort to clear away the obstacles toward meaningful, mutually satisfactory agreements.

Although we cannot forecast the degree of success which our efforts will meet, we must make the double attempt to reduce U.S.-Soviet tensions and to achieve the prevention of further spread of nuclear weapons, or face the prospect of a steady deterioration of the conditions in which peace might actually become possible on this earth.

The advance in the power of destructive weapons, the supersonic speed of airplanes and missiles, and the conquest of outer space have outmoded much of our political thinking. When nuclear weapons can destroy a large part of a nation's population and civilization in a matter of minutes or hours, what remains of isolation or distance or defenses?

We must add new dimensions to our political thought and practice in order to control what science and technology create. We must—and I, for one, believe we can—apply our best political and scientific thinking to the problems that face us, for the good of mankind. A constructive peace must be pursued even more relentlessly than our other aims. Otherwise, we shall all be condemned to exist at the mercy of a balance of terror in a world without order or security and become the victims of our unenlightened materialism.

Note on Earthquakes and Underground Explosions

The ability of science to detect and to identify otherwise unidentified seismic events by the use of distant instrumentation alone, which involves certain unresolved technical problems, might be summarized as follows:

First, it is necessary to determine what size explosion in terms of kiloton yield produces seismic signals comparable to an earthquake of a given magnitude.

Second, one must determine the average number of earthquakes above a given magnitude which occur annually in various parts of the world in order to know the number of natural events which might be confused with man-made explosions.

Third, it is necessary to determine the ability of existing and future systems of seismographs to detect (i.e., to determine the existence of) events above various magnitudes.

Finally, and most critically, it is necessary to be able to identify clearly and unquestionably the seismic event detected by the system as either a man-made explosion or an earthquake.

The size of the seismic signal received on a seismometer at a given distance from an underground explosion varies considerably with the type of ground upon which the explosion is conducted. For example, an explosion of about one kiloton yield in hard rock, such as granite or salt, would give a seismic signal equivalent in size to an earthquake in the seismic magnitude of 4. However, if an explosion is conducted in a substance of dry, porous material, such as dry alluvium (sand, gravel, and earth), then a yield of about 10 to 20 kilotons might be required to produce a seismic signal the same size as a Magnitude 4 earthquake.

Since seismic magnitudes are by definition measured on a logarithmic basis, a Magnitude 5 event is approximately ten times as large as a

Magnitude 4 event. A magnitude of 4.75 is accordingly equal to explosions with yields ranging between 5 and 50 kilotons, depending upon the type of soil in which the explosion is conducted.

Seismologists say that dry alluvium is rarely found in the world in sufficient depths to make it useful for conducting underground tests of 50 kilotons. An explosion of this size in depths of the alluvium normally available would either vent into the atmosphere or form a very visible crater.

One of the difficulties is to determine the precise seismic magnitude of any specific underground nuclear explosion. The signals from the explosion must pass through the earth along a variety of routes with different geological characteristics to reach various detection stations. The experience of seismologists has shown that for the same event the size of the seismic signals can vary by a large factor as they are received at different locations around the world.

For this reason there is likely to be difficulty in achieving agreement on the seismic magnitude of a given explosion between the scientists reading seismometers in our country and those reading seismometers in another country. That is why any unsupervised moratorium on all underground tests having a seismic signal below 4.75 is unrealistic. There might be continuous and constant arguments as to whether a particular event was above or below the figure agreed upon in the moratorium.

There is also considerable variation in the geographical distribution of earthquakes in different parts of the world. Certain areas of the world have far more earthquakes than others. Some of the areas with the greatest number of earthquakes are located in a belt surrounding the Pacific Ocean, extending from Chile northward through California, across the Aleutians, and down the Kamchatka Peninsula and the Kuriles to Japan, and finally to the Philippines and Indonesia. Another belt extends along the southern borders of the Soviet Union from the Kamchatka Peninsula to the Black Sea.

As stated in the text (pages 40-43, above), other areas such as the central U.S.S.R. and central United States rarely have earthquakes of any great size. Furthermore, there is considerable variation from year to year in the number and size of earthquakes within the U.S.S.R. Our information now indicates that annually there will occur on the average about 250 earthquakes with magnitudes greater than 4, and that the number of such earthquakes decreases very rapidly as the size goes up. Thus at magnitudes greater than 5 there would on the average be approximately only fifty earthquakes per year in the U.S.S.R., which would be distributed between the seismic and nonseismic areas.

There has been a great deal of confusion about the difference between detection and identification. Detection of seismic events depends upon the ability to record on the seismometer a signal which can be observed above the usual seismic conditions and distinguished from background noises. Present world-wide seismic systems are capable of detecting a large fraction of events with a magnitude greater than 4. This would apply equally to earthquakes and to possible underground explosions above that yield which might take place.

LASA is an array of about 525 seismometers, spread in a pattern extending 700 miles. The installation of a network of approximately ten to twelve large-aperture seismic arrays (LASA) around the world, complete with other scientific improvements resulting from the Western seismic research programs over the past few years, would be expected to improve this detection capability by as much as five to ten times. Thus the detection threshold of a future seismic system could approach the magnitude of 3 (namely, could detect signals from explosions equivalent to around a few hundred tons of energy).

But detection alone is not enough; for, after an event has been detected, it is necessary to determine whether the event was a natural earthquake or a man-made explosion. Identification requires a larger seismic signal than is needed for pure detection purposes. At the detection threshold of a seismic system, when the seismic signals from an event are just barely observed, the identification capability is essentially zero.

This capability gradually improves as the size of the signal increases to a point approximately ten times greater in magnitude than the detection threshold; thereafter the capability remains essentially constant.

Thus, for a future network of seismic arrays with a detection threshold below Magnitude 4, the identification capability will gradually increase from near zero at the threshold up to about 80 per cent for events at Magnitude 4. Thereafter—and this is important—additional increases in the magnitude of an event will not permit the system to identify much more than 80 per cent of the events. No seismic criteria are presently known by Western scientists which permit the identification of explosions as such by seismic systems at remote locations, namely, those distances which might be involved with separate "national" monitoring systems, because some earthquakes produce seismic signals which cannot be distinguished (that is, identified) at long distances from those produced by man-made explosions.

On the other hand, man-made explosions do not produce signals which are unique to explosions and which are not also characteristic of some earthquakes. Although the Soviet Union has frequently asserted the contrary, it has never presented any data to alter this conclusion despite repeated requests to do so, and Western scientists have no basis for believing that such Soviet data exist.

There are three criteria, however, which are useful in identifying at least some earthquakes. First, if the depth at which the signal originates is great, it could be concluded that the event was an earthquake since it would be impractical to carry on an underground nuclear explosion at depths of many kilometers. If the force of the signals is shallow, then it would be either an earthquake or a man-made explosion and some additional criteria must be sought to provide actual identification.

The second criterion employed is that of the complexity of the seismic signal received from the event. In general, man-made explosions are simple phenomena in which the energy is propagated outward instantaneously in equal amounts in all directions from a single-point source. Thus one might naturally expect man-made explosions to provide relatively simple seismic signals at all stations and in all directions from the point of the explosion.

Natural phenomena such as earthquakes, on the other hand, are complicated phenomena. The energy is generated over a specific area and time by periods, so that it is not propagated in all directions in equal amounts from a single-point source. Therefore the seismic signals from earthquakes might be expected to be more complicated than those from man-made explosions and to vary in their pattern in different directions. Experimental data have shown that most earthquakes do indeed give more complex signals than most explosions, but it is a controversial point whether small earthquakes, particularly those at shallow depths, do produce the same type of signals or directions as do man-made explosions. Therefore, while the complexity criterion is useful in eliminating some earthquakes as being possible man-made explosions, there are still some which just cannot be differentiated from man-made explosions.

Finally, a third criterion involves the detection of the first motion (namely, a positive or negative initial impulse) made by the seismic signal on the recording received from an underground event. Man-made explosions generate only positive (complexional or outward) first motion in all directions, while some, but by no means all, earthquakes produce negative (rare fractional or inward) first motions in some directions. Hence, if signals in some directions have a negative first motion, an earthquake rather than an explosion must have occurred.

Unfortunately, for geographical reasons a large fraction of the earthquakes in the Soviet Union do not provide negative first motions at long distances from the source of the earthquakes, and "national systems" or monitors which can operate only at those long distances and not from stations within the U.S.S.R. can only occasionally use this criterion.

By combining all three of these identification techniques, or criteria, and by building a world system of ten or twelve large seismic arrays, Western scientists believe they would be able to achieve the identification of approximately 80 per cent of all natural earthquakes at Seismic Magnitude 4, as was stated by Mr. William C. Foster, the Director of the Arms Control and Disarmament Agency, on September 2, 1965.* This leaves about 20 per cent of all natural events as well as any possible man-made explosions which cannot be distinguished one from the other. As Mr. Foster stated, even some in this 20 per cent might be identified as earthquakes if more precise information were available and the exact place of origin were known.

Such information might be obtained by the placement of ocean-bottom seismometers to provide data on whether the seismic event was in the ocean, and therefore clearly an earthquake, or on shore, and therefore either an earthquake or a man-made explosion. For the remainder of unidentified seismic events, however, some other method is needed to provide reliable information as to what caused them.

Unless some form of reassurance (namely, from a few on-site inspections) can be obtained that these remaining unidentified seismic events are not man-made explosions, then each one of them could become the source of a suspicion that a treaty banning underground tests had been violated. If there were no method set up in the treaty to give this reassurance, such suspicion would only increase tensions, and the proposed treaty would become an unstable instrument.

In summary, there is no presently known seismic method of identifying a man-made explosion as such at the distances which are feasible for the operation of "national systems."

Seismology is capable of identifying a large proportion of seismic events as natural earthquakes, but some earthquakes will still give signals indistinguishable from man-made explosions. For these, some other identification method is needed.

Our scientific inspection techniques are relatively simple and will provide the additional evidence required to identify underground

* ENDC/PV.229.

nuclear explosions as such. The United States knows of no other techniques (seismic or otherwise) which can be used for this purpose, and thus far the Soviet Union has not provided any specific suggestions or evidence to support its assertions that there are such techniques which do not require the reassurance that could be provided by a few on-site inspections of otherwise unidentified events.

Index

Aiken, Frank, 108
Akalovsky, Alex, 40, 41, 42, 86
Albania, 81
Amchitka Island, 103
Armour, Norman, 3
Arms control, and limited disarmament, 79-80; unilateral measures, 80; *see also* Disarmament
Arms Control and Disarmament Agency (ACDA), U.S., 5, 9, 62, 92, 110
Ashby, Sir Eric, 15
Atom-free zones, 54, 60, 73, 126-127; *see also* Rapacki Plan
Atomic energy, peaceful uses, 60, 92, 98, 110, 125-126
Atomic Energy Commission (AEC), U.S., "Plowshare" program, 98; views on test ban, 87

Bakhmetieff, Boris A., 1-4
Barghoorn, Frederick, 56
Bechhoefer, Bernard G., 8, 24
"Bomber bonfire," 51, 79, 114-115
Borodin, M., 1
Brazil, 13
Briand, Aristide, 1
Brzezinski, Zbigniew, 70
Budgets, exchange of military, 118
Bulgaria, 13
Burma, 13
Bush, Vannevar, 16
Byelorussian SSR, 82

Cambodia, 81
Canada, 13, 65
Chalfont, Lord, 121

Chang Tso-lin, 1
Chen Yi, 129
Chiang Kai-Shek, 1
China, People's Republic of, 4, 5, 9, 67, 69, 77, 81, 124, 128, 129-131, 136, 137, 138, 170; non-participation in disarmament agreements, 11-12, 81, 99, 106; nuclear capacity of, 11, 129-130
Churchill, Sir Winston, 88
Comprehensive nuclear test ban, 39-42, 53, 60, 87-90, 97, 102-106, 127; *see also* Inspection; On-site inspection; Partial nuclear test-ban treaty
Conference on the Discontinuance of Nuclear Weapons Tests, 5
Conferences on the Law of the Sea, 5, 7
Congo, 81, 110
Coolidge, Calvin, 4
Cuba, 81, 137
Cyprus, 110
Czechoslovakia, 13, 39, 126-127

De Gaulle, Charles, 121
Delivery vehicles, liquidation of, 75-78, 114, 129; prospects for agreement, 114; U.S. and Soviet proposals, 75-78; verified freeze on, 115
Disarmament, aims of, 67; argument against unilateral measures, 65; arms control and, 79-80; a big-power problem, 10-12, 14, 43, 65; chronology of U.S. and Soviet actions in 1964, 111-112; conditions for, 65-69; diplomats' role in, 10, 14, 88; economics of, 64, 108-109, 113;

Disarmament *(continued)*
future of, 57-62, 69, 111-119, 135-138; military strength and, 25, 65-67, 110; need for clearly elaborated agreement, 67-68; and non-aligned states, 12, 13, 30, 36, 65, 66-67, 95; and political environment, 12-14, 18, 58-59, 65-66, 67-68, 71-72, 107, 135-138; principle of balance in, 66, 68, 74; requirements, 69-72; scientists' role in, 10, 14-17, 88; U.S. and Soviet drafts on general and complete disarmament compared, 72-78; *see also* Atom-free zones; Inspection; On-site inspection; Partial nuclear test-ban treaty; Rapacki Plan

Disarmament Commission (UN), 114-115

Dodd-Humphrey resolution, 91

Dominican Republic, 110

Dooman, Eugene, 3

Dulles, John F., 86

Earthquakes; *see* Seismic events

Eighteen-Nation Disarmament Committee, 13, 29, 30, 36, 39-40, 66, 74, 95, 96, 111; co-chairmen meetings (1962), 36-43

Eisenhower, Dwight D., 86, 90

Erler, Fritz, 135

Ethiopia, 13

European Atomic Energy Community (Euratom), 110, 125

Fisher, Adrian C., 86, 92

Fisk, Dr. James B., 14, 87

Fissionable materials, cut-back in production, 111-113, 115; transfer to peaceful uses, 47, 60, 109-110, 115-116, 125-126

Foster, William C., 9, 12, 86, 116

France, 4, 5, 9, 13, 69, 121, 127, 128; non-participation in disarmament agreements, 11, 81, 91, 106

General and complete disarmament, 8, 24-27, 64, 68; *see also* Disarmament

Geneva Conference on Laos (1961-1962), 37

Germany, 38-39, 121-122, 132-133, 136-137; unification and NATO, 133-134

Germany, East, 81-82

Germany, West, 126-127, 133-135; aspiration for nuclear capability, 120-121

Gilpatric, Roswell, 85-86

Gomulka Plan, 126-127; *see also* Rapacki Plan

Gromyko, Andrei, 73; on delivery vehicles, 76-77

Guinea, 81

Halperin, M. H., 80

Harriman, Averell, 86, 91

Herter, Christian, 74, 86

"Hot-line" agreement, 19, 63, 79, 80, 92

India, 13, 67, 110, 125

Indonesia, 128

Inglis, D. R., 15

Inspection, automated control stations, 53; of budgets, 59, 114; inspectors' role in, 51, 53, 61, 94-95, 118; international, 50-54; of production records, 59; reciprocal, of closed plants, 115; Soviet opposition, roots of, 54-57; *see also* On-site inspection

International Atomic Energy Agency (IAEA), 110, 111-112, 120, 125-126; inspection of U.S. nuclear reactor, 59-60; and transfer of fissionable material to peaceful uses, 116

International Disarmament Organization (proposed), 51, 117

Israel, 110, 125

Italy, 13

Johnson, Lyndon B., 6, 111, 128; opens U.S. reactor to inspection, 59-60; on proliferation, 122

Joint Anglo-American Memorandum on control stations, 95

Joint House and Senate Committee on Atomic Energy, 87

Joint Statement of Agreed Principles, 27, 30-33, 74

Kaysen, Carl, 86
Keeney, Spurgeon, 87
Kellogg, Frank, 1, 4
Kellogg-Briand Pact, 1-3
Kennan, George F., 123
Kennedy, John F., 5, 9, 25, 41, 47, 48, 72, 78, 84, 86, 87; calls for end to atmospheric testing, 90; joint appeal with Macmillan on testing, 90; private correspondence with Khrushchev, 91; and proliferation of nuclear weapons, 120; reassessment of U.S. disarmament policies, 78; speech at American University, 91; on test ban, 42, 83, 88; UN disarmament speech, 25-26
Khrushchev, Nikita, 31, 44, 48, 61, 72, 84, 117, 135; on moratorium, 89-90; and On-site inspection, 41-42, 53; and partial test ban, 91; private correspondence with Kennedy, 91
Kistiakowsky, George B., 87
Kuznetsov, V. V., 38, 40, 41, 42, 45

Lall, Arthur, 36
League of Nations, 4
Lefever, Ernest W., 108
Leghorn, R. S., 15
Lilienthal, David E., 18

McCloy, John J., 5, 24, 26, 32, 47, 78, 86; and formation of ACDA, 9; letter to Zorin on inspection, 33
McNamara, Robert, 129, 133; approves of comprehensive test ban, 87
McNaughton, John, 86
Macmillan, Harold, 44, 90
Malaysia, 124
Mark, David, 86
Menon, Krishna, 36, 90
Mexico, 13
Middle East, 128
Moch, Jules, 75
Mori, Sir Kengo, 1, 2
Moscow Treaty, *see* Partial nuclear test-ban treaty
Mosely, Philip E., 43

Multilateral force (MLF), need for U.S. review, 132-135; and proliferation, 132-135; *see also* North Atlantic Treaty Organization (NATO)

Negotiations, advantages of informal meetings, 35, 39, 43; balancing national interest, necessity of, 10; characteristics of successful, 47; diplomats' role in, 10, 14, 88; East-West approaches to, differences in, 92-93; honesty in, 45-48; necessity for continuing, 61, 120, 138; patience in, 78; reasons for, 20-27, 30; scientists' role in, 14-17, 88; semantic problems, 24; Soviet misuse of, 90; *see also* U.S.S.R., diplomatic style and tactics
Nicholson, Sir Harold, 48
Nigeria, 13
Nine-Power Treaty of 1922, 3
North Atlantic Treaty Organization (NATO), French challenge to, 113; need to revitalize, 132-135; and U.S.S.R., 73, 98-99, 117, 122, 126, 127, 132; *see also* Proliferation
Nuclear weapons, proliferation; *see* Proliferation
Nuclear weapons in outer space, 19, 63-64; Resolution Against the Placing of Nuclear Weapons in Space, 79

On-site inspection, 39, 40, 41, 51, 97; co-chairmen meetings, 39-43; and comprehensive test ban, 39, 102-103; logistical difficulties of, 62; psychological and political factors, 104-105; Pugwash Statement, 15; purposes of, 42; Soviet opposition, roots of, 54-57; Soviet views, 41, 53-54, 93, 95-96; U.S. views, 40, 42, 53-54, 94-97; *see also* Vela project
"Open Door Policy," 3
Organization of American States, (OAS), 13, 110

Pact of Paris, 1
Pakistan, 67
Partial nuclear test-ban treaty, 6, 9, 33, 58, 63, 79, 83-84; aims, 99; co-

Partial nuclear test-ban treaty (*cont.*) chairmen's meetings on, 36-43; limitations of, 85-86; negotiations, 86-97; provisions, 97-102; reasons for Soviet interest, 10, 58, 61, 84-85, 91-92, 101; U.S. accepts risks of, 82-83, 100; U.S. proposes, 90; verification risks, 52; violations of, 99; withdrawal from, 99-100; *see also* Scientific progress

Peace-keeping institutions, 4, 52, 64, 69; control of, 71; Soviet views on, 70-72; U.S. views on, 71, 107-108

Poland, 13, 39, 126-127

Popper, David, 86

Press, Frank, 82

Proliferation, 102, 120-138; agreements not requiring inspection, 60; and "Atoms for Peace," 126; enforcement of agreement on, 125; and MLF, 132-135; NATO and, 121, 131-132; necessity of Chinese agreement, 128-129; necessity for treaty on, 120-121, 122, 123-124, 137-138 non-nuclear states and, 124, 127-130; partial nuclear test-ban treaty, 99; political environment, 122-123, 131-135; U.S. Draft Treaty, 17, 121

Pugwash Statement, 15

Rapacki Plan, 39, 60, 126-127

Report of the Committee on Arms Control and Disarmament, 104

Report of the Committee on the Economic Impact of Defense and Disarmament, 109

Resolution Against the Placing of Nuclear Weapons in Space, 79

Rhodesia, 110

Rich, A., 15

Rumania, 13

Rusk, Dean, 47

Saudi Arabia, 81

Schelling, T. C., 79-80

Schumacher, Kurt, 45

Scientific progress, and changes in verification requirements, 21, 22, 50, 53, 60, 94, 96-97, 103; exchange of information on, 118; research programs and, 109-110; *see also* Seismic events; Vela project

Scoville, Herbert, 87

Seismic events, detection through distant instrumentation, 139-144; need for joint research efforts on, 94; in U.S.S.R. mapped, 40; *see also* Onsite inspection; Scientific progress; Vela project

Shidehara, Baron, 1

Soviet Draft Treaty on General and Complete Disarmament Under Strict International Control, 27, 51, 72, 75; aimed at unilateral Soviet advantage, 66, 73; compared to U.S. draft, 72-78; and delivery vehicles, 77-78; provisions for inspection, 51

Special Committee on the Proliferation of Nuclear Weapons, 6

Spiers, Ronald, 86

Steele, Charles C., 86

Stevenson, Adlai, 114

Sukarno, 124

Sweden, 13, proposal for "non-nuclear club," 127-128

Teller, Edward, 15

Ten-Nation Disarmament Conference, 6, 13, 30

Test-ban, *see* Comprehensive nuclear test-ban; Partial nuclear test-ban treaty

Tsarapkin, Semyon K., 38, 42, 73, 76, 89

Tyler, William, 86

Ukrainian S.S.R., 82

Underground tests, *see* Inspection; On-site inspection; Seismic events; Vela project

Union of Soviet Socialist Republics, "agreement in principle," 45-46, 68, 73; diplomatic style and tactics, 19, 20, 23, 32, 34-36, 43-48, 101; domestic pressures, 21; fear of Germany, 38, 132-133, 136; military secrecy, 55; moratorium on underground tests, 93; national interests, 21, 136-137; and NATO, 73, 98-99, 117, 122,

Union of Soviet Socialist Rep. (*cont.*)
126, 127, 132; resumes nuclear
weapons testing, 90; troika proposal, 6, 19, 72, 89; and U.S., future
relations with, 135-138; *see also* Delivery vehicles; Disarmament; Inspection; NATO; Partial nuclear
test-ban treaty
United Arab Republic, 13
United Kingdom, 4, 5, 6, 13, 36, 39,
73, 74, 76, 121, 124; fear of Germany, 121-122, 133; research on disarmament in, 23
United Nations, 4, 5, 12, 13, 25, 63,
76, 84, 110, 113, 116, 137; action on
Soviet moratorium violation, 90;
future role of, 71, 72, 108; limitations as a forum, 43; peace-keeping
activities, 108
United States, and Communist China,
130-131; diplomatic style and tactics, 46; domestic objections to disarmament, 26, 88; domestic views
on test ban, 87-88; future relations
with U.S.S.R., 135-138; military responsibilities, 110, 129-130, 132-135;
and NATO, need for review of policy on, 132-135; nuclear reactors
and IAEA inspection, 59-60, 111-
112; relations with Western Europe,
134-137; research on disarmament,
23-24, 63; and War Propaganda

Resolution, 28; *see also* Delivery
vehicles; Disarmament; Inspection;
Partial nuclear test-ban treaty
U.S. Draft Outline of a Treaty on
General and Complete Disarmament in a Peaceful World, 24-27,
66, 67, 75; compared to Soviet
draft, 72-78; delivery vehicles, 75-78;
peace-keeping forces, 71; proportionate arms reduction, 73
U.S. Report to the UN: Economic and
Social Consequences of Disarmament, 108

Vela project, 15, 102, aim of, 96-97;
and inspection, 60, 95; satellites, 21-
22; and seismic events in the
U.S.S.R., 40
Verification, functions of, 50; *see also*
Inspection; On-site inspection;
Scientific progress; Vela project
Viet-Nam, 18, 81, 84

Wadsworth, James J., 5, 73, 86
War Propaganda Resolution, 19, 27-30
Wciler, Lawrence, 86
Wiesner, Jerome, 41, 42, 87, 104

York, Herbert, 104

Zorin, Valerian, 28, 29, 30, 31, 33, 37

COUNCIL ON FOREIGN RELATIONS

Officers and Directors

PUBLICATIONS

FOREIGN AFFAIRS (quarterly), edited by Hamilton Fish Armstrong.

THE UNITED STATES IN WORLD AFFAIRS (annual). Volumes for 1931, 1932 and 1933, by Walter Lippmann and William O. Scroggs; for 1934-1935, 1936, 1937, 1938, 1939 and 1940, by Whitney H. Shepardson and William O. Scroggs; for 1945-1947, 1947-1948 and 1948-1949, by John C. Campbell; for 1949, 1950, 1951, 1952, 1953 and 1954, by Richard P. Stebbins; for 1955, by Hollis W. Barber; for 1956, 1957, 1958, 1959, 1960, 1961, 1962 and 1963, by Richard P. Stebbins; for 1964, by Jules Davids.

DOCUMENTS ON AMERICAN FOREIGN RELATIONS (annual). Volume for 1952 edited by Clarence W. Baier and Richard P. Stebbins; for 1953 and 1954, edited by Peter V. Curl; for 1955, 1956, 1957, 1958 and 1959, edited by Paul E. Zinner; for 1960, 1961, 1962 and 1963, edited by Richard P. Stebbins; for 1964, by Jules Davids.

POLITICAL HANDBOOK AND ATLAS OF THE WORLD (annual), edited by Walter H. Mallory.

INTERNATIONAL POLITICAL COMMUNICATION, by W. Phillips Davison (1965).

MONETARY REFORM FOR THE WORLD ECONOMY, by Robert V. Roosa (1965).

AFRICAN BATTLELINE: American Policy Choices in Southern Africa, by Waldemar A. Nielsen (1965).

NATO IN TRANSITION: The Future of the Atlantic Alliance, by Timothy W. Stanley (1965).

ALTERNATIVE TO PARTITION: For a Broader Conception of America's Role in Europe, by Zbigniew Brzezinski (1965).

THE TROUBLED PARTNERSHIP: A Re-Appraisal of the Atlantic Alliance, by Henry A. Kissinger (1965).

REMNANTS OF EMPIRE: The United Nations and the End of Colonialism, by David W. Wainhouse (1965).

THE EUROPEAN COMMUNITY AND AMERICAN TRADE: A Study in Atlantic Economics and Policy, by Randall Hinshaw (1964).

THE FOURTH DIMENSION OF FOREIGN POLICY: Educational and Cultural Affairs, by Philip H. Coombs (1964).

AMERICAN AGENCIES INTERESTED IN INTERNATIONAL AFFAIRS (Fifth Edition), compiled by Donald Wasson (1964).

JAPAN AND THE UNITED STATES IN WORLD TRADE, by Warren S. Hunsberger (1964).

FOREIGN AFFAIRS BIBLIOGRAPHY, 1952-1962, by Henry L. Roberts (1964).

THE DOLLAR IN WORLD AFFAIRS: An Essay in International Financial Policy, by Henry G. Aubrey (1964).

ON DEALING WITH THE COMMUNIST WORLD, by George F. Kennan (1964).

FOREIGN AID AND FOREIGN POLICY, by Edward S. Mason (1964).

THE SCIENTIFIC REVOLUTION AND WORLD POLITICS, by Caryl P. Haskins (1964).

AFRICA: A Foreign Affairs Reader, edited by Philip W. Quigg (1964).

THE PHILIPPINES AND THE UNITED STATES: Problems of Partnership, by George E. Taylor (1964).

SOUTHEAST ASIA IN UNITED STATES POLICY, by Russell H. Fifield (1963).

UNESCO: ASSESSMENT AND PROMISE, by George N. Shuster (1963).

THE PEACEFUL ATOM IN FOREIGN POLICY, by Arnold Kramish (1963).

THE ARABS AND THE WORLD: Nasser's Arab Nationalist Policy, by Charles D. Cremeans (1963).

TOWARD AN ATLANTIC COMMUNITY, by Christian A. Herter (1963).

THE SOVIET UNION, 1922-1962: A Foreign Affairs Reader, edited by Philip E. Mosely (1963).

THE POLITICS OF FOREIGN AID: American Experience in Southeast Asia, by John D. Montgomery (1962).

SPEARHEADS OF DEMOCRACY: Labor in the Developing Countries, by George C. Lodge (1962).

LATIN AMERICA: Diplomacy and Reality, by Adolf A. Berle (1962).

THE ORGANIZATION OF AMERICAN STATES AND THE HEMISPHERE CRISIS, by John C. Dreier (1962).

THE UNITED NATIONS: Structure for Peace, by Ernest A. Gross (1962).

THE LONG POLAR WATCH: Canada and the Defense of North America, by Melvin Conant (1962).

ARMS AND POLITICS IN LATIN AMERICA (Revised Edition), by Edwin Lieuwen (1961).

THE FUTURE OF UNDERDEVELOPED COUNTRIES: Political Implications of Economic Development (Revised Edition), by Eugene Staley (1961).

SPAIN AND DEFENSE OF THE WEST: Ally and Liability, by Arthur P. Whitaker (1961).

SOCIAL CHANGE IN LATIN AMERICA TODAY: Its Implications for United States Policy, by Richard N. Adams, John P. Gillin, Allan R. Holmberg, Oscar Lewis, Richard W. Patch, and Charles W. Wagley (1961).

FOREIGN POLICY: THE NEXT PHASE: The 1960s (Revised Edition), by Thomas K. Finletter (1960).

DEFENSE OF THE MIDDLE EAST: Problems of American Policy (Revised Edition), by John C. Campbell (1960).

COMMUNIST CHINA AND ASIA: Challenge to American Policy, by A. Doak Barnett (1960).

FRANCE, TROUBLED ALLY: De Gaulle's Heritage and Prospects, by Edgar S. Furniss, Jr. (1960).

THE SCHUMAN PLAN: A Study in Economic Cooperation, 1950-1959, by William Diebold, Jr. (1959).

SOVIET ECONOMIC AID: The New Aid and Trade Policy in Underdeveloped Countries, by Joseph S. Berliner (1958).

RAW MATERIALS: A Study of American Policy, by Percy W. Bidwell (1958).

NATO AND THE FUTURE OF EUROPE, by Ben T. Moore (1958).

AFRICAN ECONOMIC DEVELOPMENT, by William Hance (1958).

INDIA AND AMERICA: A Study of Their Relations, by Phillips Talbot and S. L. Poplai (1958).

NUCLEAR WEAPONS AND FOREIGN POLICY, by Henry A. Kissinger (1957).

MOSCOW-PEKING AXIS: Strength and Strains, by Howard L. Boorman, Alexander Eckstein, Philip E. Mosley and Benjamin Schwartz (1957).

RUSSIA AND AMERICA: Dangers and Prospects, by Henry L. Roberts (1956).